How to Give Up Alcohol for a Month

John Hinton

Illustrations by Colin McIntyre

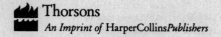

Thorsons
An Imprint of HarperCollinsPublishers

Thorsons
An Imprint of HarperCollins*Publishers*
77–85 Fulham Palace Road
Hammersmith, London W6 8JB
1160 Battery Street,
San Francisco, California 94111–1213

Published by Thorsons 1997

10 9 8 7 6 5 4 3 2 1

Text © John Hinton 1997
Illustrations © Colin McIntyre 1997

John Hinton asserts the moral right to
be identified as the author of this work

A catalogue record for this book is available
from the British Library

ISBN 0 7225 3289 X

Printed and bound in Great Britain by
Caledonian International Book Manufacturing Ltd, Glasgow

Contents

For Gay and Nick

Acknowledgements

With thanks to Dr Diana Courtney; Professor Donald Naismith, Head of the Department of Nutrition and Food Science at King's College, London University; members of Alcoholics Anonymous and the Chemical Dependency Centre; librarian Roy Johnson and his helpful research staff at Alcohol Concern in London.

Useful facts and insights were gathered from a variety of sources. Particularly helpful were the following: *On the Demon Drink* by James Robinson (Mitchell Beazley, 1988); *Loosening the Grip, a handbook of alcohol information* (Mosby Medical Press, USA, 1991); *Moderate Drinking* by Audry Kishline (Crown); *Alcoholics Anonymous*, the AA handbook; *Understanding Alcohol* by Jean Kinney and Gwen Leaton (Mosby Medical Press, 1982); *A Great and Growing Evil, the medical consequences of alcohol abuse* by the Royal College of Physicians (Tavistock, London and New York, 1987); and *The Courage to Change* by Dennis Wholey (Fontana, 1986).

Thanks also to many drinking and non-drinking friends; to the journalists who often write on alcohol, not always with tongue in cheek; to doctors, psychiatrists, psychologists, counsellors on addiction and others. And last but not least, thanks to my old Dad, whose special fruit punch of cider, gin and Cointreau made parties of fond memory quickly get into top gear but who, himself, always knew when to give it a rest.

Foreword

As the millennium dawns, health has become big business. You only have to look around you. Bookshops give us healthy living through dieting, exercise, alternative medicine. Supermodels star in videos exhorting us to become fitter. There's a health club around every corner, and every school-child knows that smoking can kill. Even the government has produced a Master Plan for the Health of the Nation.

But what about alcohol? Its potential as a lethal weapon is well known, yet society can't get enough. Pubs are open all day, supermarkets tempt us even on a Sunday and no social occasion is complete without a glass of something celebratory. As a subject, drink has become an art form deeply in-grained in popular culture from Sinatra to Oasis.

As a general practitioner doing my bit to promote the health of the nation, one of the main stumbling blocks is getting people to admit they might drink a little too much. It is a taboo subject – surprisingly so in this 'no-holds-barred' age we live in.

It can be really hard to give up, even for a health-restoring month, and it's not much fun being cast in the role of a pariah. But at last help is at hand. John Hinton's book is an everyday working manual on how to give up alcohol, just for a month, without suffering insult or rejection. There are even handy hints on how to spend the time and money saved. Definitely a book to have at home and leaf through as you sip something hard – or soft. And a great helper if and when you decide to venture away from the alcoholic tides for 30 days.

As a voyage of discovery, I recommend it.

Doctor Diana Courtney, MB Ch.B.

1. The 30-Day Zero-cost Programme

Kindly have a sip of your favourite alcoholic tipple and throw away your cares. This isn't one of those revivalist programmes which claim that the end of the rainbow is only a few steps away if you discover ginseng tea, drink pints of cider vinegar or spend all your disposable income on aromatherapy and mud baths. This is a non-active, laid-back, zero-cost, chilled-out programme.

Put another way, this book is about taking nothing at all. It is about *not* taking something that you may consider to be one of life's adornments. For just a month.

The suggestion – never proposed before in a handy reference book – is to embark on a 30-day period of abstinence from mankind's favourite drug which has encouraged more howls of laughter down the years than even the combined muses of the Marx Brothers, the Goons and Monty Python. And enough tears to float the *QE2*.

A Barrel of Laughs

Funny? Do you remember that dinner party when Charles had a skinful and his head lolled until he fell asleep in the soup? And everyone just left him there and carried on talking? Funny? John shared a bottle of brandy with a mate, walked out of what he thought were the French windows to pee on the lawn – and fell nearly 20 feet. He was on the first floor; a simple error which cost him a broken foot. Funny? Working for one of the flagship television current affairs programmes, a young, ambitious reporter returned from a savage civil war with some great footage. She had a long liquid lunch, laughing and joking with colleagues about her exploits, before dubbing her commentary. That is, *trying* to dub her commentary. She couldn't do it, fluffing time and time again. Funny at first but then rather agonizing. Smashing lunch, but the hard fact is she wasn't used again.

Funnily enough, most alcohol stories involve ridiculous behaviour. (I once drove the wrong car home from a wedding.) And we like them because they show us people out of control, breaking the mould, making a spectacle of themselves. In an increasingly conformist society which insists on protecting us with railings lest we stray like brainless sheep into the road, it's a counter-balance, a reminder of our humanity. Yet another reason why alcohol will always have considerable appeal.

How Much Do We Drink?

In fact, the suggestion that you should get off the magic roundabout for 30 days is a daring – even defiant – idea since alcohol is such a ubiquitous substance. In the UK, hundreds of thousands of people are employed in the making of it, and nine out of ten adults drink it – plus a third of all children aged between 13 and 16. There are powerful forces at work keeping us drinking. Suggesting even temporary abstinence has the dull thud of financial disaster about it projected onto a nation that spends £16 billion a year on booze – more than the annual spend on clothes, schools and hospitals – of which the government gulps £9 billion in tax.

'He's trying to block out all the adverts for drink.'

Discounting television, drinking is by far the single most popular paid-for pastime in Western society. A 1994 survey carried out for no less than the Potato Chip Bureau asked men which of all the pleasures in life they would most hate to give up. Thirty-seven per cent said alcohol. That still leaves plenty of room for sex, gambling and fishing, but it's certainly worth a headline. And the fondness for alcohol has increased with post-war prosperity. In 1950, the average Briton drank 3.7 litres of pure alcohol a year. By 1990, that had doubled to 7.5 litres. And, of course, stories involving alcohol are decanted into the columns of our daily newspapers in a never-ending stream. This isn't a naming names book, but the number of showbiz and sporting personalities who have waded through the alcoholic slough of despond is legion. Just open today's paper.

Why Should You Give Up?

Give up? Take nothing? What's this all about? It's just a suggestion, mind. You could load a skip with copies of this book and padlock yourself to it but it wouldn't stop you drinking for a day, let alone 30, if you didn't want to. You would simply make a call on your mobile and have the skip towed to the nearest pub. So let's have none of this compulsion nonsense.

Your grandmother might just have died from alcoholic self-poisoning (let's hope she hasn't). Your hard-working father might have drowned the sorrows and stresses of business in Scotch, making him testy and capricious at home. But that doesn't mean you're going to end up the same way.

You're you.

However, if you have picked up this book deliberately, you may have some passing interest in the subject. What's the motivation – and the good sense – behind the decision of some to give booze a rest for one month out of the twelve; or put another way, five years out of a drinking career of sixty years?

You might think there is a strange logic to it. If you have ever worried about building-up a dependency on alcohol, here is a chance to break the chain that some people find to their discomfort has become gradually but tenaciously attached to the wine rack or cocktail cabinet or the bar of their local.

As I noted in my management handbook *Ever Onward* (Grafton, 1986) about the snares lying in wait for those who too intensively pursue the executive life: 'It is probably easier to get a divorce than to tackle a drink problem that's out of control.'

Are Drinkers Born or Made?

Do you subscribe to the disease model or the behavioural model of over-drinking? The first is based on the theory that obsessive drinking has inherited, genetic causes and can be overcome only by a commitment to abstinence, ideally shored up by membership of Alcoholics Anonymous (AA). The second is that heavy drinking is an acquired habit which can be checked by a period of abstinence after which moderate – but not daily – drinking can be resumed. This is the founding belief of Moderation Management, a new group started in the USA.

Do You Have a Problem?

If you think your drinking is out of control – and only you really know – this is not, in all honesty, the only book you should be reading. If you find the thought of giving up for 30 days really oppressive – *almost impossible to contemplate* – then you should be reading rather more serious books and taking some specialist advice. As a cautionary tale, Chapter 9 looks at some of the medical complications caused by alcohol and what you can do about them.

But don't treat this as a Bible on the dangers of drink. For many medics and other experts, booze is a lifetime study: Alcohol Concern in London has around 150 titles in its bookshop and 2000 publications in its library. If you want to know more, there's plenty available.

Keep Your Self-denial to Yourself

Okay, you *are* in control. Why not plan to stay that way by laying alcohol aside for 30 days? It's not always easy – which is why this book is designed to help. And here is the first lesson: NO-ONE IS INTER-ESTED IN YOUR 30-DAY PROGRAMME BUT YOU. NO-ONE IS LIKELY TO TAKE YOUR NON-DRINKING PROJECT SERIOUSLY. YOUR SELF-DENIAL IS ABOUT AS INTERESTING, EVEN TO GOOD FRIENDS, AS YOUR HOLIDAY SLIDES. IT SOUNDS EARNEST AND UNREWARDING, OF DOUBTFUL IMPORTANCE – OBSESSIVE, EVEN.

ER, THIS IS AN IMPORTANT POINT, SO I'LL PUT IT YET ANOTHER WAY: DON'T EXPECT YOUR FRIENDS TO HELP. THEY WILL BE BEMUSED AND MAY EVEN TRY TO CONFOUND YOUR PLANS IN THE NAME OF GOOD COMRADESHIP OR PURE DEVILMENT.

Don't count on your friends to help you.

Why Should You Want a Break from Drinking?

There are a number of reasons why you might want to stop drinking for 30 days, particularly if it's just after Christmas, or any period when you have been overdoing it. It might simply seem a good idea for all sorts of old-fashioned reasons. Among them:

- You feel just a little jaded and put it down to a personal level of consumption that's been getting a bit too regular.
- You are fed up of hangovers.
- You want to feel fresh and bright in the morning.
- You know enough about the dangers of dependency on booze to want to prove *to yourself* that you don't need it for a month.
- You enjoy drinking quite a lot but fear becoming an alcoholic (someone with 'Alcohol Dependency Syndrome' to use the latest phrase) with all the chaos and the clinics and possible purgatorial abstinence at the end of it. You know that a month's self-imposed 'cure' will be a good way of keeping things under control.
- You want to lose weight. And, boy, does alcohol put on the pounds!

This book is designed to stiffen your resolve to start at Day One and get through the course.

Note that this isn't an 'anti-booze' book. A whole society banned booze earlier this century, and whatever good Prohibition did for America, it also spawned a powerful, tenacious and malign gangster culture now feeding off drugs. Ordinary drinkers – by far the majority – get along with alcohol very well, except when they overdo it. And if they continually overdo it, they're no longer ordinary drinkers.

Prohibition wasn't a success.

Giving Up is Hard to Do

Giving up isn't easy because drink is an accompaniment to so many things. In some businesses, it is part of the process of selling products or ideas to clients, or relaxing after a hectic day, celebrating success or trying to remain cheerful if the bank's on the phone.

Socially, you can expect to be offered a drink anytime from noonish to bedtime as part of normal social intercourse – not necessarily every day but most days.

All this, of course, is obvious. Precisely. Booze *is* obvious, quite difficult not to stumble into at every turn. Wine bars, pubs and off-licences – 200,000 of them in the UK – are on every block in the best and most rundown neighbourhoods. Thanks to relaxed licensing restrictions, cans of beer, bottles of wine and ready-mixed cocktails can be bought almost round the clock at corner shops along with the morning paper, a bag of crisps and a bar of chocolate.

Booze is available at the start of every rail, sea or air journey, during the journey and at the end of the journey. It is certainly far harder to avoid than your favourite soap opera. Harder, almost, than smoking, now that smoking is prohibited in so many places. And as for sticky buns and doughnuts ... if you're concerned about alcohol's potential for putting on the flab, no doubt you'll be keeping a beady eye on those as well.

And it's not just the fact that it's at your elbow which makes a drink difficult to avoid. A drink is offered socially as a gift, a token of friendship or of welcome. It is not just lying there waiting to be plucked, which would be temptation enough; but people hand it to you, tilt the wine bottle over the glass nearest you at the table, include you in a round.

For many people trying to go 'off' for a time, this is the first hurdle. And they don't make it. Life sometimes seems short enough of encouragement, and turning down a drink, in a quick emotional reaction, is a bit like spurning a friendly gesture. Almost an insult. So we'll be looking at ways to overcome this hurdle without causing offence and without provoking full-scale debate on the subject with some saying 'Very good idea' and others looking as if you've just been sick on the carpet.

Alcohol Dependency Syndrome

Why such sensitivity? It's because alcohol remains a mystery. Nine out of ten people in Britain drink. The recommended sensible limits have recently been revised slightly upwards, but in 1992 they were 21 units per week for men and 14 for women. A study carried out during that year by the Office of Population Censuses and Surveys revealed that 28 per cent of men and 11 per cent of woman exceeded this dose. Even so, most take it easy, perhaps taught by their parents or peers that alcohol is like a flame – a provider of warmth, but also capable of igniting destruction.

Roughly one in ten drinkers get burnt, becoming victims of the mysterious alcohol dependency syndrome, and the mystery is why them? The disease model or the behavioural model? The debate continues to rage about the exact causes of 'alcoholism' and the best treatment for it ... but there is no debate about the fact that it does hit – and hit hard. Indeed, could you become dependent on alcohol? Whatever else is involved, it stands to reason that the regularity and scale of drinking is the main cause of the symptoms which cause the misery. One disturbing statistic, quoted to me by a member of AA, is that of the ten per cent who 'catch' the disease, only one in ten fully recovers; the rest submit to various mental and physical maladies.

That alcohol can trigger clinical depression is well known, and its ability to help you 'deal' with a difficult situation – marital problems, a financial crisis – is illusory. Perhaps less well known is that 30 per cent of people in the UK who take their own lives abuse alcohol. (In the USA the figure is 40 per cent.)

The cloud of alcohol at the end of the known universe.

Why are some people more prone than others to getting the alcohol bug in earnest? The real answer is that while astronomers have discovered the huge cloud of alcohol at the end of the known universe, earthbound doctors have not yet drawn into focus the full answer as to what makes an alcoholic. Nor have pharmacologists discovered a 'moderation' pill, let alone a hangover cure.

That many alcoholic suicides have been talented, creative and very good company only deepens the mystery. There is only one rational explanation: that their addiction to alcohol skewed their lives, stunned their talent and made their lives unbearable. Ernest Hemingway is the classic example. As the American writer, Donald Newlove – a recovering alcoholic – observes: 'Nobody dies for poetry or art. You *live* for poetry. You suicide out of misguided self-pity.'

Those who turn down a drink for even a short time are casting an eye of suspicion on alcohol, and by their action admitting it has a dark side. Others may not want reminding of that, particularly if they are enjoying the party and the freedom from inhibitions and cares which alcohol provides ... or grimly hanging on to a habit they cannot break. (Approached at his local by a drinking companion who had gone on the wagon, Hemingway grimly moved to the other end of the bar.)

There is a feeling – if only in your imagination – that by turning down a drink, you are spoiling the fun. So you have a drink, don't you? Well, no you don't. Not for 30 days you don't.

ᵠᵠ

A drunkard is like a whisky bottle, all neck and belly and no head.

Austin O'Malley

ᵠᵠ

2. What You'll Be Missing

No other legal substance on earth accompanies as much pleasurable activity as alcohol.

It is not, or is rarely, the *raison d'être* for a gathering but it adds to the enjoyment for those who want to drink a fine wine with a meal, raise a glass in a toast, share the glow of a brandy with an old friend.

'It's my security blanket – I just like to know it's there.'

No point in trying to hide it – you may miss drinking for 30 days.

You may miss the subtle and implicit conspiracy between companions of the bottle; the taste of a good wine; the warm parade of a liqueur down the gullet and into the stomach; the feeling of being in the 'swim'.

You may miss the first plunge of mouth and nostrils into a nutty pint of Real Ale and the refreshment of those first few gulps, leaving a rime or 'head' round the glass.

You may miss the refreshing bite of a cold glass of white wine and the way it complements, for instance, smoked salmon and brown bread.

You may miss the delicious, gassy taste of an ice cold lager as a cooler *par excellence*.

You may miss the sweet, cloying taste of a good port balancing the tang of a ripe Stilton.

You may miss the confluence of lemon, tonic and gin in a G & T.

You may miss a glass of robust claret accompanying roast beef and all the trimmings.

Yes, you may miss all this. But not, perhaps, as much as you think.

IN ANY CASE, IT IS NOT FOREVER. IN FACT IT IS PRECISELY TO AVOID THE HORRORS OF A 'TOTAL' BAN THAT YOU ARE GIVING IT A REST FOR 30 DAYS. AND THAT EVEN INCLUDES THE UNEXPECTED CELEBRATORY GLASS OF CHAMPAGNE OFFERED WHEN YOU LEAST EXPECT IT. WHICH MEANS IF YOU WIN THE LOTTERY

WITHIN THE 30-DAY PERIOD, YOU HAVE A COKE.

And remember one more thing you'll be missing: the hangover. Almost worth giving up for that alone.

♉♉♉♉♉♉♉♉♉♉♉♉♉♉♉♉♉♉♉♉♉♉♉♉♉♉♉♉♉♉♉♉

'Thank you, my man. And could you bring me a large gin and tonic?'

Bernard Falk to the ticket collector on the Paddington to Reading commuter service.

♉♉♉♉♉♉♉♉♉♉♉♉♉♉♉♉♉♉♉♉♉♉♉♉♉♉♉♉♉♉♉♉

3. The Importance of a Positive Attitude

Remember, there is no compulsion about this programme. The 30 days is neither a prison sentence, nor a punishment you have devised for yourself. You are exercising – you could say celebrating – a basic freedom *not* to do something.

Remember – it's not a life sentence.

Case Histories

John, a financial PR man, subscribes to the annual abstinence programme for all the right reasons. But possibly out of self-consciousness, a desire not to appear a killjoy, he makes it appear heavy weather.

'God, it's so boring,' he said in the midst of an alcohol-free Lent. 'I'm so boring.' Did he mean it? We were having a splendid full English breakfast. He was bright-eyed, replete with fresh grapefruit juice and good humour and giving his scrambled eggs no quarter. Brimming over with confidence, he would later try to win his prize client three or four column inches in the *Financial Times* or *Wall St Journal*. And he might well succeed.

After work, he might grow wistful at the thought of foregoing a refreshing pint of bitter, but he would overcome the temptation. Psychologists would find it hard to detect any real boredom. Instead – probing deeply – they would find a quiet pride in self-discipline, in the ability to keep alcohol at arm's length.

Here's what Sue, another abstainer – the rest of the time a moderate drinker – says about her 30 days off. 'I see it just as a need to flush the system out and show myself that I can do it. Apart from a couple of restless nights at the start, it's not painful. I'm not gasping at the end of it and I see no reason to prolong it since I take exercise and rarely have more than three glasses of wine a day.'

Now living in California, Joe, an engineer, who has practised the 30-day programme for years, says simply: 'Everywhere I go there's alcohol available – good booze at that. I give it a rest so that I can keep it in perspective. I have seen too many guys fail to reach their full potential because they have let it loom too large in their lives – always having the extra one; wanting the party to go on all night; in fact, wanting the party to go on permanently. And then the party's over and they're looking over a cliff edge.'

Sarah, an advertising executive, tried the 30-day programme as this book was going to press, reporting after seven days a fairly strong desire to have a glass or two of wine but a strong nose also for the fact that she was saving time – not just the time spent in the pub or wine bar but the consequences too: lying slumped in front of the television on her return home and getting nothing done. What had to be done she wasn't sure, but a disorganized wardrobe did spring to mind. That and, er, household chores. But the main asset, she was finding, was waking up clear-headed and the accompanying bonus of her creativity returning. 'Feeling more cheerful and getting ideas – these are real benefits,' she reports.

The big test for Jim, another abstainer, was the wedding reception he attended where the choice between alcoholic and soft drinks was made starkly clear. 'At one end of a huge, long table were flutes of champagne with attentive waitresses ready to lift them into waiting hands. At the other end were glasses of orange juice.

'I felt very exposed, as if everyone in the room was looking at me, waiting to see what I'd decide. Opting for champagne was the comfortable choice; what was this guy doing drinking orange juice? I wondered what the waitresses might think, but I finally went up to the orange juice end and asked for one. I watched the waitress's face carefully as she served me, to see what her reaction was – but actually she wasn't looking at me at all; she was looking over my shoulder at the next customer.'

Liz, a housewife, mother and mature student, subscribes to the 30-day rest period – and shorter periods throughout the year – simply because 'I feel better if I don't drink. If I drink half a bottle of wine at dinner, which I enjoy, I wake up feeling very groggy and I then feel tired throughout the day, which is no fun if you've got a lot to do. When I abstain, I wake up feeling much brighter, rewarded for having a Coke or a mineral water instead of a good glass of wine.'

Putting Your Mind to It

The *Oxford Dictionary of Quotations* has, taken together, page after page of cautions about drink. James I, whose detestation of 'the black stinking fume' of tobacco smoke was notorious, also declaimed against 'the sin of drunkenness which is the root of all sins'. And Washington Irving (1783–1859) believed that 'they who drink beer will think beer'.

Without becoming anti-drink – a lost cause if ever there was one – if you are preparing for 30 days on the water-wagon it is worthwhile shoring up your defences a bit, even if they are not intended to hold back the 'flood' forever. There is good sense in many of the bromides about booze over the years. Remember it was booze which laid low Alexander the Great soon after his 30th birthday and after he poked out the eye of his best friend in a drunken rage. So many nights of feasting and merriment – that wasn't one of them.

Attitude – a steely resolve if that's not too dramatic – is all if you are to make it through your 30-day programme. If you are tempted to play the martyr on occasions, bear in mind that no-one cares whether you are on the fifth day, thirteenth day or twenty-fourth day. TO OTHERS IT IS A MATTER OF STUPENDOUS INDIFFERENCE WHETHER YOU REACH THE 30TH ALCOHOL-FREE DAY. It is, therefore, quite gratuitous to suggest that your progress through your self-imposed dry spell is onerous, a burden to be bravely endured. If you have thrown yourself overboard while in full possession of your senses, don't ask for – or expect – sympathy.

Far better to be outwardly casual while remaining alert to the questions which could knock you off your perch early on (see Chapter 5).

'He's preparing himself for his dry-out.'

And keep in mind the 30-day programme creed:

1. Thirty days is only one month out of twelve. It will pass very quickly. And why should it be painful? That surely is to overdo the importance of alcohol in your life.
2. Quite apart from an absence of hangovers, 30 days off the booze may be beneficial medically. By all means let your doctor know you're doing it, but don't expect him to drop everything and monitor your progress.
3. To each individual drinker, alcohol dependency is a threat, however distant. It may be salutary to let it take a walk for a month.

4. It doesn't matter what people think. Most won't care a damn. Some might quietly approve. DON'T WORRY ABOUT THIS.
5. Yes! It will save money (see Chapter 14).
6. It will free up valuable time (see Chapter 15).
7. Hangover free, you are likely to feel brighter and more energetic.
8. No studies support this, but a common-sense view is that you might well live longer.
9. You might be nicer to your partner, if you have one.
10. You might just put in 99 per cent effort on a work project, rather than 75 per cent or less. And that does tend to get noticed.

♀♀♀♀♀♀♀♀♀♀♀♀♀♀♀♀♀♀♀♀♀♀♀♀♀♀♀♀♀♀♀♀♀♀♀

Drink not the third glass which thou canst not tame once it is within thee.

George Herbert (1593–1633)

♀♀♀♀♀♀♀♀♀♀♀♀♀♀♀♀♀♀♀♀♀♀♀♀♀♀♀♀♀♀♀♀♀♀♀

4. Choosing the Right Moment to Start

Try not to launch your 30-day programme off the same slipway as the usual New Year resolutions. That is, don't start on the first of the New Year and get it all muddled up with other directives to yourself. For, sadly, few resolutions last longer than a week. As Simon Davies wrote in the *Daily Telegraph*: 'As early as January 2, most of us will augment our resolutions with a variety of carefully engineered caveats. By January 3, our friends and colleagues will all agree with us that the whole resolution idea is silly. Until next year.'

So don't get your 30-day programme mixed up with anything else, such as giving up smoking. Abstaining from both alcohol and tobacco is too much to take on at once.

Take it easy. Relax. You can do it – in your own way. If you have any doubts about your general medical condition, phone your GP and let him or her know what you intend. Certainly you should let the doctor know if you develop any really uncomfortable withdrawal symptoms which may need treating – or at least talking about.

When it comes to stopping drinking for 30 days, there is, of course, nothing to do but put down the glass, cork the wine, or even – if you want to make a grand gesture out of it – throw the remains of your last drink down the sink.

But remember this programme is about *not* doing something. Do you want to dress it up as follows? Let's imagine you discuss tactics with your partner:

'As from now/tomorrow/Sunday noon/my birthday/your birthday/the next full moon/the end of the Tory Party Conference, I'm going to give it a rest for a while.'

'*How long's a while?*'

'Thirty days from now/tomorrow/Sunday noon/my birthday/your birthday/the next full moon/the end of the Tory Party Conference.'

'*Oh.*'

'Harry does it. I was talking to him about it. It sounds like a good idea.'

'*Does that mean you won't want to go out?*'

'No. But he's sure it saves him money.'

'*Are you going to put all the bottles away?*'

'Well, I thought I'd tidy them up a bit.'

'*Good. Thirty days, eh? Think you can do it?*'

'WITHOUT A DOUBT!'

And so say all of us. But really, it's a lonely decision with a deadline all of your own making. No one to compare diaries with. No one to make excuses to. And nothing really to boast about, given the strange taboo surrounding the subject.

Choosing Day One

There are always scores of possibilities for prevarication: a wedding coming up when the champagne will be flowing, a university reunion dinner, an office party, even a funeral. Depending on your social schedule or social 'whirl', there will always be a good reason to put off Day One.

And if you consistently put off Day One, you might as well abandon your 30-day programme altogether.

So adopt a bolder approach. Why not?

You could look in your diary and start on one of those days mentioned above – when it can be guaranteed that the drink will be flowing like a waterfall. A wedding party when, from noon until late at night, all you would normally have to do is stretch out your glass to have it refilled with champagne. And get thoroughly pie-eyed.

To prepare for the day, throw out any half-empty bottles of wine that may be knocking around and put the gin, whisky, sherry away at the back of a cupboard. Buy some soft drinks such as apple and orange juice and Coke and bung them in the fridge.

Then wait for the wedding day.

On Day One turn up at the reception looking bright and thinking positive, and drink mineral water or orange juice until you can drink no more. Then eat as much food as you like (the heavier drinkers tend to neglect food until much later) and then enjoy a coffee. If you feel like smoking slightly more than usual, don't worry because smoking has absolutely nothing to do with your 30-day programme. Similarly, don't feel guilty about what you eat; you are not changing your whole diet and throwing out white sugar, crisps and chocolate.

Cruise around the party looking intelligent and making witty remarks, and when you've had enough, leave. Some of the drinkers will stay longer until the champagne absolutely runs out and the

You will scintillate with wit at weddings.

departure of the bride and groom is a distant memory, then go to the pub for beer and gin and tonic, then have an expensive and forgettable meal at a wine bar. The next day, they will be profoundly hungover and wondering what hit them. While in no way being sanctimonious, you will wake clear-eyed and fit for a new day.

Mind you, you will have missed a few jokes, one or two good stories and the usual round of gossip – in which you might have figured. Torture yourself pleasurably with the thought that while you were back home hanging your trellis, others with nothing better to do were possibly impugning your character. The speculation may have been that you have a drinking problem; that you are depressed and taking some pills which don't mix with alcohol; that your mother or father or even your grandparents may have had a drinking problem; that you have had a disappointment at work; that you and your partner are about to break up; that you may have been taking other recreational drugs. And so on.

Do you care what anyone says anyway? Because the most likely scenario is that your absence will hardly be noticed.

Other preparations in the 30-day programme are simple and concern finance. The main thing is to get an up-to-date bank statement and check your balance on Day One. If you are really rigorous, keep a little notebook of the money saved each day, weddings included – don't forget the unscheduled late-night meal and share of the wine bill. Or put the money you would have spent on drink in a jar (see Chapter 14).

Giving Up with a Friend

In view of the distressing side of this journey into the non-alcoholic nether regions, it might be an idea to carry out the programme with a friend and compare notes daily on your progress. At least she will understand because she, too, is trying to reach the 30-day target. You could phone your friend after spending a whole evening in the pub without touching a drop. You could share the triumph of surviving a hen night without giving in to temptation. You could cry on her shoulder when the going gets tough.

One day at a time. And just think, in 30 days' time you and your friend will be able to change the subject.

ꝗꝗꝗꝗꝗꝗꝗꝗꝗꝗꝗꝗꝗꝗꝗꝗꝗꝗꝗꝗꝗꝗꝗꝗꝗꝗꝗꝗꝗꝗꝗꝗꝗ

A drunken night makes a cloudy morning.

Sir William Cornwallis

ꝗꝗꝗꝗꝗꝗꝗꝗꝗꝗꝗꝗꝗꝗꝗꝗꝗꝗꝗꝗꝗꝗꝗꝗꝗꝗꝗꝗꝗꝗꝗꝗꝗ

5. How to Refuse Booze

It's one thing to give up cigarettes. It's another to abstain from booze. Former smokers occupy the moral high ground, as Douglas Johnson wrote in the *Independent*. But when drink is turned down 'there is no admiration ... The distinctly horrid word "teetotal" is bandied about. It should apply only to those who are ill or who adhere to some fanatical religious faith. The abstainer does not occupy the high moral ground here; he is suspected of adopting a supercilious attitude to the rest of mankind.'

That may well be the prevailing mood towards the 'taboo' side of not drinking. But let's admit that some of the people you might meet for the first few days won't turn a hair if you order mineral water at lunchtime.

Try to read the person, but even if you know them quite well, it won't be easy to second-guess how they'll respond. When you get to the table and the waiter asks whether you want an aperitif you must, of course, order mineral water, or something

'Ein Mineralwasser, bitte.'

else soft. Your companion might not remark on this.

But they might. When the waiter trips back with the wine list he might give it to your companion at which point they will ask – reasonably enough – 'Are you having any wine?' And you say: 'No thanks – I'll stick to mineral water.'

It might be left there. Or not as the case may be. You have to be prepared for (1) some resistance, (2) some disappointment, (3) some questions.

Probably the easiest escape from the boredom of interrogation is to fit your 30-day period into the six weeks of Lent. This is a great time of Christian denial, and it makes sense to forsake booze in a gesture of solidarity towards the trials and tribulations of our Lord in the wilderness. Few will argue if you simply say with old-fashioned rectitude: 'I always give it a miss for a time over Lent. We've always done it in the family. Seems a sensible idea.'

But using Lent as an excuse is rather abusive of its religious importance. Why practise deceit just to cover your own embarrassment? Because you're going to face some questions anyway. At whatever time of year.

Resistance

'Are you sure? There's a really delectable bottle of Sancerre here, very reasonable at a tenner, and I

Lent is a good time to drop the drink.

thought we might share it. I'll buy! Completely selfish, of course, but it goes very well indeed with the seafood brioche they have on today and which I very much recommend if you haven't tried it before.'

Now that's all a bit insistent but don't be put off. If your companion is only here for the contents of that bottle – perish the thought – then they want the best part of a bottle's worth anyway – whatever you do.

'Quite sure, thanks.' Reply warmly, sincerely and firmly, offering no explanation.

Disappointment

Some will then want to register their disappointment. You have, after all, spoiled their main lunchtime plan.

'Can't get it in a half-bottle, unfortunately,' they add. 'In fact there doesn't seem to be *anything like it* in a half-bottle.'

Enough of this. 'Can't you get a decent wine by the glass?' you ask. Of course they can. Or they might throw shame to the winds and order the full bottle anyway – 'I'll just leave what I don't want' – which is no problem for you except that by the time they have finished most of the bottle, they'll be getting quite pissed and may become tiresome company.

Either way, you shouldn't feel bound to apologize. The particular bottle of wine was clearly their

Such a pity you can't join me – they only do this one in jeroboams.

treat to themselves. You had little to do with it – they admitted as much. Therefore you have clearly not deliberately spurned a real gift and actually have nothing to apologize for.

The Questions

Now you might be with one of those blissfully curious people – the natural journalists amongst us – who crave answers in a completely dispassionate way. Or you could be with someone who feels that lunch isn't lunch without a bottle of wine, who's a little surly after failing to find a drinking companion. Either way, the questions will fly since drink is a subject of never-ending fascination. C'mon, it's a hurdle, and a bit of humour will help.

'It's not like you to say no to a glass of wine.'

Now if it's lunchtime you're pretty well off the hook.

'No, I just make it a rule during the week. Wine makes me dozy in the afternoons and I rather like to stay sharp because we're pretty busy.' Or: 'Not today. I have to drive later; I'm picking up the kids from school.' A shrug, a look of resignation, even an appeal for sympathy. Anything to get the boring subject off the menu as soon as possible.

There is then the prospect of having to listen to an outpouring of guilt from your companion about his or her drinking along the lines of 'I know I should cut down myself … must get round to doing it … if only I could find a soft drink I like …' It's pretty dull stuff and not what you want to talk about over lunch. So move onto something else as soon as you reasonably can.

Dinnertime is different, of course. Here the meeting is much more social, something to be lingered over, a treat. Say you're at dinner with a group of old friends. You've already resisted an aperitif, and now the wine is being ordered. There's no avoiding it. You have to say:

'No wine for me; I'll just have the mineral water.'

'I thought we might have a bottle between us as we wait for the food. Sure you won't join us?'

'No thanks. I'll stick to mineral water.'

Any more and an explanation becomes due. Now here's where you can use the 'mysteries of medicine' ploy if you don't want to be honest. Lots of people do, viz.:

'I'm on some tablets at the moment and I'm afraid they react with alcohol.'

Or:

'I've got to watch my diet and cut out booze at the moment because of some virus I caught.'

Or:

'I'm having some blood tests at the moment and the doctor said it would skew the results.'

The trouble with these answers is that your questioner will be left with the distinct impression that you have a severe infection that doesn't bear thinking about, or that you are breathing out a killer swarm of African bugs.

You could, of course, have a bit of fun by inventing a medical card and carrying it with you at all times. Get your local instant-print bureau to do it. To be 'authentic' the card should measure 3½ x 6½ inches, have an extra colour (to black and white) to make it look serious and have TREATMENT CARD in large letters at the top.

Just bash out some doggerel on your word processor and the instant-print people will lay it out for you. This will include your name and, say, driver's licence number and the name of a drug which you can easily invent, for instance Penguinan or Puffinium. Then, in quite prominent bold letters:

'Avoid alcohol while taking this treatment.' And, of course, a medical disclaimer as a footnote: 'This card is unofficial and should not be used as a basis for treatment in an emergency.' Just in case you get run over.

This will look pretty good when you tug it out of your pocket and wave it in front of your persistent questioner.

'Just having to take some medicine for a while. Something to do with blood chemistry. Having a few tests. Here's my treatment card – looks pretty impressive, eh?'

Costs a bob or two? It should easily repay the investment with a few laughs ... afterwards.

But is there a perfect way out? Writing in *The Times Magazine*, the witty and wise Matthew Parris said he had met a man who, in a single phrase, solved the problem he had always had with refusing an alcoholic drink. Facing the inevitable 'Oh, come on, why not?', this chap replied: 'Because I like to know what's going on.' As Matthew reports: 'Immediately sounding just slightly more manly than the rest of us.'

Or how about this:

'Every year I have 30 days off alcohol so I can enjoy it the rest of the time.' And if that raises an eyebrow and the interrogator is still buzzing around, try: 'A couple of friends are now six feet under because of booze, and I have no intention of letting it get the better of *me*.'

To add a further postscript to Matthew Parris's

excellent suggestion: if someone persists beyond normal curiosity, they obviously have a morbid interest in the subject and/or are trying to embarrass you.

If the mention of dead friends doesn't pierce their inflated curiosity, try changing the subject. Glance down at their feet, look startled and say: 'God, where did you get those shoes? I've been hunting for a pair like that for ages.' Then get others to crowd round and admire the aforesaid shoes before slipping away, leaving the idiot to their embarrassment. At least they won't pester anyone else in a hurry.

The Debate

Even if you have successfully established that you are not going to drink alcohol on this occasion, you are not necessarily out of the woods. The balance of payments may be plunging downhill like a roller-coaster, business may be tough, a man in an ape suit might be climbing the Empire State Building watched by half the world's population on television. But if you are unfortunate, nothing – to the dinner companion with a gleam in their eye – will displace their interest in your non-drinking. You are a pacifist, *sans* gun, on the wild Main Street of Dodge City.

'Just wondering: I've always thought it must be a real strain not to have a drink with good food like this. Don't you miss it? You *must* miss it a bit.'

Answer: 'Yes I do miss it a bit. But the food tastes just as good. How's the wine; any good?'

'Excellent – want to try a sip? Just *half* a glass?'

Answer: 'No thanks. Put it on ice for a month and I may take you up on it.'

'I don't think I could manage a *day* without a drink, let alone a month, whatever the doctor said. Isn't he just being over-cautious?'

Answer: 'He might be. But he's the expert. I'm not really in a position to judge.'

'I mean, what could be more natural than wine? I think I'd have to be on my deathbed before I'd give it up.'

Answer: 'Well, I'm not at death's door, but if I was I'd give up wine like a shot if I had to.'

'Actually you're less likely to end up at death's door with alcohol. The studies I've read say that wine is good for the heart. Keeps everything flowing smoothly.'

Answer: 'In moderation. If you drink too much, up goes the blood pressure.'

'All I know is that my grandfather drank like a fish and smoked like a chimney and thoroughly enjoyed himself. You can get worried to death by these doctors' reports. It's enough to drive you to drink! Don't you find it *dreary* not drinking?'

There is a pause as your companion drains their glass and refills it. There is still a slight gleam in their eye. Time to close off this endless companionway to nowhere.

'Anyway,' you say, 'let's change the topic can we?

As I'm not drinking at the moment, I'd rather not talk about it all the time – unless you really want to. Just a thought, but if you really can't do without a drink every day …'

'Well …'

'How much do you get through on average? Do you know?'

The subject will very soon change. For your companion has grown too fond of their drink. They won't want any questions about themselves and what has become their favourite companion. You may disturb them. It's a problem, but not one you can deal with.

'*Ever had a check-up? You could have an enlarged liver. Do you still get hangovers? When you start not getting hangovers any more is when you have to start worrying.*'

NO ONE SHOULD MAKE YOU FEEL GUILTY ABOUT NOT HAVING A DRINK.

♀♀♀♀♀♀♀♀♀♀♀♀♀♀♀♀♀♀♀♀♀♀♀♀♀♀♀♀♀♀♀♀

No good and worthy man will insist upon another man's drinking wine … They who submit to drink as another pleases, make themselves his slaves.

Dr Johnson

♀♀♀♀♀♀♀♀♀♀♀♀♀♀♀♀♀♀♀♀♀♀♀♀♀♀♀♀♀♀♀♀

6. The Alternatives to Booze

To the drinker used to the kick of alcohol, nothing will ever completely replace the tang of lager, the crispness of white wine, the bite of a vodka and orange, the malty taste of a pint of English bitter or the aromatic nose of a good whisky.

Out of the huge selection of soft drinks available, a non-alcoholic ginger beer perhaps comes the nearest by delivering a kick to the back of the throat, closely followed by a fierce Virgin Mary made with a teaspoonful of Tabasco. And many soft drinks will give you a 'lift': Coke's famous lift results from a good dose of sugar and caffeine. And what's wrong with that?

You can drink it – and all the other soft drinks – night and day and it won't provoke an indiscretion or inflame your temper.

It was with this in mind that wines, spirits and beer were forbidden by the promoters of the Great Exhibition of 1851. But vast numbers of people drank lemonade, ginger beer, seltzer water and soda-water, all supplied by Messrs Schweppes.

'An amusing little number from Tesco, made with Tuscany lemons with more than a hint of effervescence.'

Lest you despair of finding a fruity or other-flavoured soft drink that's to your liking, there are also a dizzying amount of mineral waters to choose from. Here's a checklist of soft drinks and waters to be getting along with:

- Coca-Cola – the 'real thing', whatever that means. Certainly the original cola, and tastes best by far out of a glass bottle.
- Britvic orange – always delicious but one is never enough.
- Idris or Schweppes ginger beer – a gutsy first impression with a soapy aftertaste.

- Schweppes tonic water – 'Shall I take my iron?' inquired the wet-looking golfer. 'Aye, and yer quinine,' retorted the fierce Scottish caddie.
- Lucozade – the reassuring energy boost for athletes and invalids.
- Rose's Lime Juice – part of the great English seagoing tradition. Try it as a 'short' over the rocks with just a small amount of water.
- Robinson's Barley Water – a very good squash maker.
- Irn Bru – formerly Iron Brew, claimed by Glaswegians to possess restorative properties.
- Tizer – let your schooldays roll around your tongue.

And the spring waters:

- Evian
- Volvic
- Contrex
- Vittel
- Perrier
- Benoit
- Malvern
- Vichy
- Buxton
- Highland Spring

Many of these now have subtle fruit flavours, and are less 'up front' than conventional sodas. There's certainly a good selection to choose from over your

30-day period. And non-alcoholic cocktails can also be fun, if you can be bothered to make them. For recipes, pop along to your local bookshop.

'Ginger ale and mango juice – shaken not stirred.'

ΩΩΩΩΩΩΩΩΩΩΩΩΩΩΩΩΩΩΩΩΩΩΩΩΩΩΩΩΩΩΩΩΩΩΩΩ

Water is the only drink for a wise man.
                    Henry David Thoreau (1817–62)

ΩΩΩΩΩΩΩΩΩΩΩΩΩΩΩΩΩΩΩΩΩΩΩΩΩΩΩΩΩΩΩΩΩΩΩΩ

7. A Man's 30-Day Programme Scenario

Here, from a man's perspective, might be a typical non-drinking scenario with some of the obstacles likely to be encountered as you march on, soft drink in hand, towards the 30-day objective. For a woman's scenario, see Chapter 8.

'Better keep an eye on Jenkins for the next few days.'

Day 1

This is a good idea, isn't it? Don't even think about not pressing on – you've only just started! You are engaged on a month-long programme that's going to improve your health, possibly your temper *and* your bank balance. So start putting the money you save into a jar.

Day 2

Some people might stumble but not you! If you have a slight gnawing feeling in your guts, treat yourself to a bar of chocolate. And there is nothing wrong with Coca-Cola; it's only water, sugar and some other stuff which has never been targeted as a serious health risk. Keep it cold – and drink it!

Day 3

So Rachel is leaving and having a few drinks after work tonight. Go! Just don't get caught in a big round – why should you pay for everyone else's drink when you're on mineral water or Coke? Just refuse (in the nicest possible way), and if anyone scoffs, remember that they don't really care all that much whether you drink or not. If anyone persists, say you're doing a 'Soberthon' for charity. Or use the blood tests ploy (see page 37).

Day 4

You are throwing a dinner party. Prepare a delicious dinner, chill your Coca-Cola and an acceptable bottle of wine and stick to the Coke. If your guests bring two bottles of wine, let them have as much as they want. If their behaviour starts to get a bit over the top, hint that it's time for them to leave by looking at your watch.

Day 5

A breakfast meeting. You are functioning like clockwork. Here, indeed, is one of the benefits of giving up the booze.

Day 6

Business is stressful, but you are enjoying the challenge. There's a presentation to write/dictate with all sorts of figures and research to build in. You break the back of it with ease, and though you don't finish until 8.30 p.m., it's well done. Had the wine been broken open shortly after six, God knows what time you would have got home.

Day 7

How nice it would be to celebrate the first week of your 30-day programme with a glass of … no.

Day 8

By plane to attend a conference. The air hostess glides into view with the usual offer of pre-lunch drinks and your colleague opts for a gin and tonic with almost indecent haste. You would normally ask for a Bloody Mary with a stick of celery, Tabasco, salt and pepper, slice of lemon – the whole caboodle. You do and you don't: you have a Virgin Mary, complete with Worcester Sauce but leaving out the ounce of vodka. And, actually, it tastes quite good. And you didn't miss the vodka all that much, did you?

Day 9

Over to see your parents. As dinner approaches, Dad reaches for The Famous Grouse. You decline. Does he look crestfallen? Has his son become a sobersides? Don't worry – he's lived long enough not to worry about you going on the wagon for a while. And as for the claret at dinner, well, there's more for him. One thing about Dad, and many drinkers of his generation, is that they can tie one on at Christmas and weddings and funerals then leave it alone for weeks. And Mum is delighted because, in her experience, booze creates more pain than happiness.

Day 10

You play golf – 36 holes – with an old friend who quite likes to stop for an hour-long lunch in the locker bar and have two to three pints with his Cornish pasty, Scotch egg and tongue sandwich. You have non-alcoholic ginger beer and there are no questions because, to the golfer, nothing is more interesting than the game at hand – one of the reasons why it is so relaxing and addictive. The result: you play the after-lunch 18 holes with rare skill, only losing one ball, achieving two pars and a birdie. You also manage to maintain an even temper with your golf trolley which, after two or three pints, normally takes on a malign life of its own, crashing over like a runaway wheelchair. You win the match.

Day 11

The 40th birthday of a friend with all due ceremony. Some of the guests are there just to make an appearance. Others get stuck in for a long evening. In all the happy milling around, your non-drinking isn't noticed. But at dinner, amongst some senior wine drinkers, you're glad you have purchased a copy of this book and rehearsed your questions and answers (see Chapter 5). After dinner, you accept a noisome cigar, puffing smoke about like Thomas the Tank Engine and generally looking devilish and worldly-wise. Even so, you pass the port … yes you do.

Day 12

Your firm is having a press conference. Even though many journalists these days hardly stay long enough to grab the press release – and don't have time to down even a coffee – it has been decided that refreshments will be laid on with a trowel. One or two more senior reporters tarry after the presentation and make a very good fist of the smoked salmon and Bucks Fizz. Rather tired of dealing with remarks about non-drinking, you fill up a flute glass with orange juice, tear into the smoked salmon and don't let on. And a jolly time is had by all – including you.

Day 13

You may find that this is one of those days when alcohol's presence is so muted as to be forgettable. You have a sandwich at your desk; no-one is leaving or joining or celebrating at work, nor is there anything remotely sociable planned for the evening. And the thought of booze just never enters your head.

Day 14

To avoid lunch at the wine bar (because the wine is considerably better than the food), you have a sandwich and then go and enjoy an hour at a gallery. On the way back to work, you buy the latest best-seller by Michael Crichton or Tom Clancy, and read the whole story that evening ... or until 2.30 the following morning.

Day 15

Wake feeling short of sleep but, in other respects, very refreshed. Reflect that after the best part of a bottle of wine, you wouldn't have finished the book. And you would very possibly have had a headache. Congratulations – you're halfway through the programme.

Day 16

Check your money jar. Depositing in the glass jar with reasonable accuracy the money you would otherwise have spent on drink, you now have £150. Do you spend some of it? That's up to you. However, there is a sale of Italian shoes – reduced from £145 to £55 – that is of immediate interest. A pair of mouth-watering loafers plus the latest Robert Harris novel in hardback would still leave you with about £80. What a tempting prospect.

Day 17

You join some friends for dinner out of town. Usually there would be an irritating cloud hanging over the gathering: how much wine are you going to chance given the drive home and the threat of the Breathalyser? This time there are no worries. What happens is that another couple decide to abandon their car until the next day and accept a ride with you. Any comments about you not drinking are muted. It is enthusiastically suggested that you continue the experiment.

You will achieve sudden popularity – as a driver.
'Could have sworn I lived here – must be the next village.'

Day 18

You have been dissatisfied with your bank for some time. Having spent more time than usual on your own admin. at home, you are pleased to receive an introductory pack you sent away for from a competitor. Comparing their rates and services, you fill in the necessary forms and post them back. Nothing like a positive decision.

Day 19

Work is okay, but one or two things are troubling you and you are slightly cheesed off. The monthly meeting today has a faintly dispirited air; the team is troubled. Without even contemplating anything immediate, you resolve to brush up your CV.

Day 20

In the pub after work, someone suggests a low-alcohol lager. You turn it down. Then the suggestion turns to an alcohol-free lager, but you have tried this and found it slightly sweet with a metallic aftertaste. Instead, you have a ginger beer mixed with lemonade in a pint glass: certainly a thirst-quencher.

Day 21

You post your CV to a recruitment agency. At this stage of the programme, you have ceased to think about alcohol at all. How much alternative activity does alcohol displace? The many-sidedness of your life is becoming more apparent.

Day 22

With the shoes and the Robert Harris novel still a tempting prospect, you now have well over £200 to spend or save.

Day 23

A new client has to be royally entertained to lunch. Avoiding French and Italian cuisine, you opt for a Japanese blowout where the accompanying drinks don't have to include sake and wine. He does drink, sparingly, and doesn't even mention your own choice of Aqua Libra. And the food is mouth-watering.

Day 24

An evening out with your wife/girlfriend. There is no alcohol exclusion zone for her, so a drink first, then a movie, followed by a Chinese meal with which you have tea. No wine tastes good with hot and sour soup.

Day 25

A colleague asks whether you will start drinking again once the 30 days are up. An interesting question. One businessman of your acquaintance had to give up during a spell in hospital for a minor operation and never started again. 'Just decided not to bother,' he said. It's an interesting question.

Day 26

A business trip to Milan where a veritable banquet is preceded by trays groaning with Negronis – a delicious and deadly cocktail of gin and sweet vermouth. You pass – as do quite a few others. The evening meal is splendid but you have never liked heavy Italian wine. The fact that you pass – in fact upturn your glass to avoid the attentions of the wine waiters – and drink sparkling water is hardly noticed, certainly not made into an issue. You are also careful to pass on the chocolate mousse which is loaded with liquor.

Day 27

Flying back from Milan. Probably the most difficult drinks to avoid are those served on an airliner. Something to do with the 'out-of-this-world' feeling of being eight miles up; the feeling of being pampered; the suspension of reality, the ... Hang it, No! You do not spoil your record at this point.

Day 28

Opening the medicine cupboard at home by mistake, you notice that you have not had occasion to call on the analgesic properties of paracetamol, aspirin or Alka-Seltzer during the past month. It comes as quite a shock – a pleasant shock.

Day 29

You notice that you have lost weight from around the waist. Another benefit, though it was not the main object of the exercise. Not a lot in a month – probably half a stone – but enough to be seen sideways in the mirror.

'Five ... four ... three ... two ...'

Day 30

Your determination has paid off. You have managed the not inconsiderable feat of avoiding alcohol for 30 days. You now deserve:

- a box of chocolates
- theatre and dinner
- or a large one.

It's completely up to you.

The glow of clear-mindedness comes back and there is a shine in my blood that beggars all my old drinking dreams.

Donald Newlove

8. A Woman's 30-Day Programme Scenario

Sipping sherry at home is one of the slippery slopes for the lonely housewife, and for some the temptations of the afternoon 'wine and video' party beckon. For working women, there is the alcoholic side of work and home entertainment to avoid if they want to embrace the 30-day programme and its benefits.

Day 1

There's a reception at work to celebrate a merger with another company. Champagne, Bucks Fizz and straight orange are on offer. A bit difficult to tell the orange from the Bucks Fizz, and you find yourself asking the waiter if he's *sure*. The orange is cloying after a few glasses, and straight mineral water seems rather dull. Not a good start.

Day 2

A day free of temptation apart from the half-bottle of Frascati left in the fridge with only a rubber stopper between you and a crash very early on in the race. You pour away the remains of the Frascati and note that other bottles in the wine rack are pleasantly dust-covered and in a strange way less susceptible to a raid.

Day 3

According to medical science, you are now free of alcohol – all having been expelled from the system. But there is a drinks party tonight with a few friends, some of whom are quite capable of seeing off a bottle and a half each without turning a hair.

Day 4

The party wasn't so bad. One of the guests had just been operated on for cancer. There was no talk of your month-long break from booze as a result. However fatal booze problems can become unless checked, you are determined not to become a booze bore. You join in the mingled hilarity and disquiet as Jackie, having falling asleep in the loo, has to be dragged out to a taxi. Jackie's doing this rather a lot lately.

Day 5

Mother is coming to stay, and as your 'ban' can hardly extend to her, you drop in at the off-licence for a bottle of whisky and a bottle of gin. And some rioja.

Day 6

As expected, on arrival, mother is naturally expecting a large gin and tonic, then another, then wine with dinner and a whisky afterwards. Your own sobriety is initially treated with amusement then a certain amount of shock as it becomes clear you mean what you say.

Day 7

The following day – the reason for mother's visit – is a family christening which, as usual, entails champagne, sangria and beer all the way. You find some consolation at the nursery bar with a stiff orange and lemon squash. The day is marred by mocking comments from family members, such as: 'Did the doctor *order* you to give up?' and 'How can you possibly bear it?' An unpleasant young cousin of 14, nursing a pint of bitter, observes: 'Been overdoing it, eh?'

Day 8

The next day, visiting relatives gather *en massc* for a Mexican dinner. Alcoholically, most opt for bottled beer. Asking for Coke, you receive the flattish variety from the fountain. When will people learn that Coke is best served straight out of its traditional glass bottle?

Day 9

Today a colleague at work decides to start her own 30-day programme. You visit a wine bar together and drink mineral water like conspirators.

Day 10

You discover Rose's Lime Juice which, poured over ice with just a splash of mineral water, has the sharp flavour that eludes most soft drinks.

Day 11

You had almost forgotten you had a blender – though it's clearly more difficult to make up your own drink than it is to open a bottle. Try a blend of lime and lemon juice with just a spoonful of sugar. Delicious. And, of course, if you buy a large variety of fruit you can fill up some wide-necked bottles with the result.

Day 12

An invitation to the cinema. And whatever the characters do on screen, an evening free of temptation.

Day 13

A weekend conference with, as usual, more hospitality than work, beginning with the opening reception. You start as you mean to go on with Perrier, or perhaps one of the snappier Italian waters. Not shimmering in a champagne flute but in a chunky glass with plenty of ice and a big slice of lemon for some flavour.

Day 14

One delegate said with mild surprise, 'What, no champagne?' Your liquid intake otherwise escaped comment.

Day 15

To Paris on Eurostar, a trip that combines business and pleasure and – gulp – no alcohol.

Day 16

To be in the megalopolis of wine and not drink is a contradiction in terms. Console yourself with the thought that there must be many Parisians who don't drink, even if there are others who bathe in the stuff.

Day 17

Next leg of the trip includes the champagne caves of Épernay. This, of course, has historic interest, seeing the dust-covered bottles ripening in the dark. But then there are the post-tour tastings which are difficult to resist. Here it is in front of you. Shall you taste it? Well, no, you don't. But, by God, it's an effort.

Day 18

Aren't eighteen days, including a visit to the home of champagne, enough. Would a sip or two matter? Well …

Day 19

But you stay steady. Today.

Day 20

And today. You just keep feeling fresher and brighter.

Day 21

And another day. Now you are starting to feel more confident.

Day 22

A friend has invited you to a concert in a church. Unknown to you, this is to be followed by a hearty bash in the crypt which would put most wine bars to shame. You are herded with others on to a jolly table where wine bottles start arriving in unholy quantities. There is one bottle of mineral water between six. You grab your share, but when the mineral water is finished it is not replaced, and towards the end of the evening you are distinctly thirsty. And, of course, you don't complain.

Day 23

Twenty-three days! Must be a record. Of course it is. Since the age of eighteen – and a bit before that if we are being pedantic – hardly three or four days have passed without you having an alcoholic drink.

Day 24

Effects? You notice that you are sleeping more soundly and awaking refreshed with more energy.

Day 25

According to your sexual partner, this aspect of life has also taken a turn for the better.

A drink before and a cigarette afterwards.

Day 26

A friend invites you to a wine tasting but this really is one you have to turn down.

Day 27

Is the burden starting to lift with only three days to go? You wonder about stocking up with wine and asking a few friends round to celebrate.

Day 28

Should you launch again into the alcoholic seas? Worth thinking about.

Day 29

You can, at least, ask a handful of friends round in a few days on a bring-your-own-bottle basis. Even if you've then finished your self-imposed exile from alcohol, you don't have to start again if you don't want to.

Day 30

Ah, achievement! And if you can do it once, you can do it again.
   You now deserve:

- a box of chocolates
- another trip to Paris
- and?

9. The Medical Overview

The medical position on booze appears to bob up and down like a cork on the proverbial wine lake. And it's not all bad news. We are told that moderate amounts of alcohol are good for the circulatory system, clearing potential blood clots; that the relaxing effects induced by alcohol can be a useful counter to stress; and that wine aids digestion.

The beneficial effects of alcohol are, however, based on an adherence to a safe level of intake which would make many drinkers despair. What's safe? On average, men drink one and a half pints of beer or three glasses of wine each day, and women one glass of wine. But the average is formulated from figures that take into account those who never drink alcohol at all. Young adults exceed this average by 50 per cent. Heavy drinking is five to seven pints of beer a day or up to fourteen glasses of wine – that's two standard bottles. And that's almost certainly trouble on the way, possibly sooner than you think.

Moderation lies, of course, somewhere in between. According to Department of Health guidelines in the UK, that's two to three pints of beer or four to six glasses of wine for men and half that quantity for women. *Not every day but two or three times a week, allowing gaps for the alcohol to be totally vacated from the system.*

Alcohol hits women harder than men because only 45–55 per cent of their body weight is made up of water, compared to 55–65 per cent in men. So, in men, the intake is significantly more diluted.

How Alcohol is Absorbed

Where does the intake go? When alcohol arrives in the stomach, it triggers secretion of hydrochloric acid, causing a warm sensation. In 10–20 minutes the alcohol is absorbed into the bloodstream through the stomach wall and the small intestine, and is then carried to the brain. The less food there is in the stomach, the greater the feeling of intoxication. The strength, or proof, of the drink also affects how intoxicated you will feel. The initial mental effect is the depression of inhibition – usefully turning off self-consciousness and timidity in those so afflicted – followed by the slowing down of co-ordination and reactions to intellectual or physical challenges. Marshalling an argument gets tough; so does operating a word processor.

Barely one tenth of the alcohol taken on board is eliminated from the body in urine, respiration and sweat. The rest is oxidized; like food, it joins with the oxygen in the blood to release heat and energy (or calories).

The cupful of raw alcohol present in every 12-per-cent bottle of wine is processed by the liver very slowly, at a rate of one unit per hour. This function cannot be accelerated by huge draughts of water, Alka-Seltzer, strong tea or black coffee or, well, anything. Whatever you do, it just sits in line in the bloodstream waiting to be 'done'.

Nor does the presence of large amounts of alcohol in the system make the liver work any faster. It doesn't turn up a dial. Nor does furious exercise – drawing on the high calorific content of alcohol – increase the metabolism. The unmetabolized alcohol has to queue up in the bloodstream waiting for processing, however much you wish it wouldn't. And it is the presence of alcohol in the blood, and therefore the brain, which keeps you inebriated. One bottle of wine takes seven hours to be processed, so it is perfectly possible after a heavy session to be pie-eyed the following morning.

The Effects of Heavy Drinking

Push the intake well beyond the guidelines and up goes the blood pressure and on go the pounds. Not to mention the possibilities of the ill-chosen word, the unfounded allegation, the flaring temper, the clumsy breakage of plate or glass, the childishness. In some people who have overdone it too regularly, reached the end of the drinking rainbow and beyond, the anger doesn't rise. Instead one sees depression – alcohol is, of course, a depressant of the central nervous system – and perhaps they need to take more than a month off.

Can Drinking Be Healthy?

But what about this 'good for the heart' business? The Royal College of Physicians has decided that middle-aged people who drink small amounts have a lower rate of coronary heart disease than those who don't drink at all. This benefit does not apply to young men, or to women who have not yet reached the menopause. However, doctors do not recommend *starting* to drink to help the heart because the benefit is quickly negated if consumption goes up. The Royal College of Physicians states in a report that: 'After three drinks a day for men, two for women, any reduced risk of CHD is overshadowed by increased risk of death resulting from accidents and violence, certain cancers, liver cirrhosis and haemorrhagic stroke. For these and other alcohol-related causes of death, the risk grows with alcohol consumption. And, in women, even moderate drinking may increase the risk of breast cancer.'

ΩΩΩΩΩΩΩΩΩΩΩΩΩΩΩΩΩΩΩΩΩΩΩΩΩΩΩΩΩΩΩΩΩΩΩΩΩΩ

'Tis pity wine should be so deleterious,
For tea and coffee leave us much more serious.

Lord Byron

ΩΩΩΩΩΩΩΩΩΩΩΩΩΩΩΩΩΩΩΩΩΩΩΩΩΩΩΩΩΩΩΩΩΩΩΩΩΩ

10. What Lies Ahead for the Heavy Drinker?

Here's mud in your eye. Heavy drinking can provoke a catalogue of illnesses:

- stomach disorders, including gastritis, bleeding and ulcers
- depression and other psychiatric and emotional conditions
- high blood pressure
- vitamin deficiency
- sexual difficulties, including impotence in men and frigidity in women
- brain damage
- muscle disease
- problems with the nervous system – especially nerve pains in the arms and legs
- hepatitis (inflammation of the liver) and cirrhosis (permanent scarring of the liver)
- cancer of the mouth, throat and gullet
- additional problems for people with diabetes

Oh, and premature death.

Alcohol may temporarily suppress fear, but fear of alcoholic-related illness is well founded and is by far the most valid reason for taking a month-long break. Alcoholism is one of the most common chronic diseases, affecting 7 per cent of the population. Treated early – but do the patients *want* to be treated? – it can be completely cured, but the cost of a return to normality is abstinence. Untreated, the secondary medical complications loom up large, since nearly every organ is affected and there is every possibility of a fatal outcome.

Here are just some of the problems that can be produced by heavy drinking year in, year out.

Digestive Problems

Moderate amounts of alcohol can disturb the normal functioning of the gastrointestinal system – the route by which alcohol enters the body and is absorbed. But heavy use of alcohol can play merry hell.

Why? A lot of booze stimulates the secretion of hydrochloric acid by the stomach lining, inflaming the lining itself. It also hinders the muscular contractions that pass food along the intestines. Combined, these effects irritate the mucous membrane lining the gut, especially the stomach. It can also cause the pyloric valve, which controls the passage of the stomach's contents into the small intestine, to stick in the closed position.

The results can include breaking wind, loss of appetite, violent nausea, retching and vomiting and alternating diarrhoea and constipation. If severe, the stomach irritation can produce inflammation, abdominal pain, gastritis and internal bleeding

Pancreatitis

Pancreatitis – a relapsing illness primarily associated with alcohol abuse – causes nausea, vomiting, diarrhoea and severe abdominal pain. It can also lead to diabetes.

The job of the pancreas is to manufacture digestive juices needed to break down starches, fats and proteins. These are secreted into the duodenum through the pancreatic duct.

There are two beliefs about the effects of heavy alcohol intake on this part of the digestive system. The first is that the pancreatic duct can become swollen if the small intestine is irritated by alcohol. No longer able to pass through it freely, the digestive juices are bottled up, inflaming the pancreas. The second theory is that additional fats in the bloodstream produced by heavy drinking end up in the pancreas and are digested by enzymes designed to break down dietary fats. The products of this process – free fatty acids – cause cell injury in the pancreas, in turn releasing more fat-digesting enzymes and creating a vicious cycle.

Liver Disease

Breaking down alcohol, which starts with a liver enzyme called alcohol dehydrogenase, is a job that receives high priority. But this is an organ with a lot to do (such as manufacturing blood-clotting factors, storing some vitamins, regulating the blood sugar level), and liver disease occurs when excess alcohol disturbs its metabolic machinery and throws its normal working off balance. There can be three results:

1. Fatty Liver

Any heavy drinker – not necessarily an alcoholic – should beware of this. What happens is that deposits of fat build up in normal liver cells because of a decrease in the breakdown of fatty acids and an increase in the synthesis of fats by the liver – distracted, in effect, by the amount of time it is spending processing alcohol. A symptom of the condition is a jaundiced appearance. Acute fatty liver occurs when between one third and one half of dietary calories are being provided by alcohol, even if the rest of the diet is sensible. The good news is that fatty liver is a reversible condition if the patient stops drinking.

2. Alcoholic Hepatitis

This is a more serious condition, again found in non-alcoholics as well as alcoholics. More often than not, it follows a fairly long 'session' of heavy drinking – perhaps a particularly bibulous festive season. The condition involves inflammation of the liver and some damage to liver cells, and the liver's metabolism is seriously disturbed. Jaundice is a tell-tale sign: the yellowish colour of the skin and the whites of the eyes comes from a pigment found in bile, a digestive juice made by the liver, when it is out of control and circulating in the bloodstream in excessive amounts.

Other symptoms can include weakness and fatigue, loss of appetite, occasional nausea and vomiting and mild weight loss. In some patients it is completely reversible provided they stop drinking. Alcoholic hepatitis is often – but not always – a forerunner to cirrhosis. About 20 per cent of those who do stop will go on to develop alcoholic cirrhosis. This compares with the 50–80 per cent risk taken by those who continue to drink.

3. Cirrhosis of the Liver

The most notorious physical manifestation of very heavy alcohol consumption involves the wholesale destruction of liver cells and their replacement by useless scar tissue. True, there are different types and causes of cirrhosis, but long-term heavy alcohol use is by far the predominant factor. One in ten long-term heavy drinkers will eventually 'catch' the disease.

Many of the abnormalities produced are irre-versible. The liver is unable to cope with the normal blood flow. Toxins circulate in the bloodstream with consequences to almost all parts of the system. Half those affected will also develop pancreatitis. The overall treatment includes abstinence from alcohol, multivitamins, bed rest and a well-balanced diet. But there are no 'miracle cures'.

For those diagnosed as having cirrhosis yet who continue to drink, the prognosis is predictably bad. One study showed that half the number of those newly diagnosed who continued to drink were dead within five years.

And once they were just eighteen and having one or two with their friends …

Effects on the Blood

Each of the major elements of the blood – including red cells, white cells and platelets – are significantly affected by heavy alcohol intake.

Red blood cells are produced by the bone marrow but its ability to process iron (a key ingredient) is, it is generally believed, inhibited by excess alcohol. Or the iron intake may simply be deficient – the result of an inadequate diet. Red blood cells can also be lost through gastrointestinal bleeding.

Heavy boozing also affects white cells which form one of the body's main defences against infection. In effect, it depletes their number by having a toxic effect on white cell reserves, meaning that fewer are available to kill invading bacteria.

Alcohol also decreases the number of platelets, a major part of the body's clotting system, by having a toxic effect on their production in the bone marrow. The result: heavy drinkers bruise and bleed more easily.

The Alcoholic Heart

Abnormal heart rhythms (arrhythmias) are, more often than not, attributable to alcohol. These include irregular patterns, often with a beat more rapid than usual. There are also irregular contractions of the lower part of the heart – a condition which can cause sudden death. Arrhythmias tend to happen after a boozy holiday or a weekend binge.

On the upside, when it comes to the cardiovascular system, it is now thought that a couple of drinks a day may protect people *without blood fat abnormalities* against heart attacks. This it does by causing increased levels of high-density lipoprotein cholesterol and lower levels of low-density lipoprotein cholesterol.

So, a little of what you fancy …?

Conversely, a definite link has been established between heavy drinking and hypertension – raised blood pressure – which is bad news. Heavy drinkers should have their blood pressure checked from time to time. Strokes, which are closely related to hypertension, are three times more common in heavy drinkers.

The Kidneys

The kidneys, unusually, are not directly affected by alcohol. But because other systems are affected, and specifically a hormone which regulates water retention, they can cease to reabsorb water to meet the body's needs. This happens when the blood alcohol level is rising. When it's falling, the opposite is true. This can lead to urinary tract infections and/or prostatitis.

Reproductive System

The release of inhibitions, which is the key to alcohol's enduring popularity, can produce heightened sexual interest, but the ability to translate thought into deed can often be frustratingly stymied – with either partial or complete impotency in men.

Alcohol can shrink the testes, leading to a drop in the level of the sex hormone, testosterone, in men. In women, there may be missed periods and an effect on the ovaries. The Royal College of Physicians says 40–90 per cent of heavy-drinking men report loss of libido with 25–50 per cent becoming more potent after giving up drink.

Alcohol in Pregnancy

Heavy-drinking during pregnancy can lead to infants being born with foetal alcohol syndrome. Alcohol passes through the placenta, hindering prenatal development. A typical baby with this syndrome will be smaller than average, in both weight and height. The head will be small, due to inhibited brain growth. The facial appearance may be unusual. At birth, the baby will be tremulous, as though suffering from withdrawal symptoms.

The syndrome does not result simply from chronically heavy drinking by the mother. Moderate and regular social drinking can also do the damage. Here is a useful daily table:

Less than two drinks	very little risk
Two to four drinks	10 per cent risk of abnormalities
Ten drinks	50 per cent risk of abnormalities
Over ten drinks	75 per cent risk of abnormalities

And because the unborn baby has to go drink for drink with mother, yet has an undeveloped enzyme system, he or she will have a higher concentration of alcohol in blood and tissue than Mum.

Respiratory System

Moderate amounts of alcohol increase the respiration rate. In very large doses the rate can be slowed, which can cause breathlessness in people with chronic pulmonary disease.

Glands and Hormones

Overdoing alcohol can cause hormonal imbalance through its effect on the 'boss' gland – the pituitary – and others which it controls. Hand in hand with this may go the problems of a damaged liver, unable to metabolize hormones as it should.

Neuropsychological Impairment

Do heavy drinkers eventually lose their marbles? Well, yes, in a way they do. It takes a long time, but regular heavy drinking eventually takes its toll. The IQ may remain relatively normal but defects do develop: a decreased ability to solve problems, to perform complex psychomotor tasks and to use abstract concepts.

Abstinence brings considerable improvement after only two to three weeks. Further improvement is seen over the next six months to a year. It is thought, however, that these improvements, although robust, are not complete.

In studies carried out in America, it has been noted that much of the impaired functioning is subtle, not readily apparent. Many of the patients in the clinical studies seemed normal: 'young, intelligent and looking much like any other citizen'. The conclusion is that such alcohol-related brain damage may be more widespread than previously thought.

The Nervous System: Dependence and Addiction

Of all the major organ systems, the central nervous system (CNS) is the one most comprehensively battered by heavy drinking.

The main acute effect of a skinful on the CNS is that of a depressant. Alcohol is not a stimulant; it is the depressing of inhibitions that makes it seem so. Relaxation comes first. Then, free of restraint, behaviour can flourish that would otherwise be suppressed. Acutely intoxicated people are in a state of mild delirium.

To the onlooker, it may appear that those undergoing the experience are having a great time. And perhaps they are. There may be a flow of ideas, laughter, bizarre connections made between one subject and another, clumsiness and clowning around. Medically, what is happening is that caution is being thrown to the winds, thinking has become fuzzy and recent memory blurred. The only trouble is that having gone through the 'fun' stage, some people can then relapse into a state of resentment, bad temper, character assassinations and tears: the intemperate moods of a fractious child.

Heavy drinking in many cases leads to physical dependence and addiction, which is something everyone wants to avoid – and none more so than those who both enjoy the taste of alcohol and its effects.

Tolerance

Developing a tolerance to alcohol is the unhappy consequence of too many, too often. Changes take place that affect the way the body metabolizes alcohol and alter its impact on the nervous system. It's a bit like drinking weaker stuff since there is both an increased rate of metabolism of alcohol and a decrease in impairment for a given blood alcohol level. (The non-tolerant individual will continue to become intoxicated at the same rate.)

As tolerance marches on, larger amounts of booze are necessary to get the desired effect, which has been described as a 'click' in the brain – the door closing on discomforting reality.

Tolerance is a remarkable demonstration of the ability of the body – and the nervous system – to adapt and function normally, despite a regular intake of booze. Tests show that if the dose of alcohol which led initially to high blood alcohol levels is held constant, the blood alcohol level can decrease, as can the clinical evidence of intoxication. And if the blood alcohol levels are raised slowly, hardly any signs of intoxication can be seen. All very curious. And we have no idea why. The basis for this metabolic tolerance has not been established.

Having built up a degree of tolerance to large amounts of liquor, heavy drinkers can sometimes develop reversed tolerance. Now everything changes. With only a couple of drinks, they are well gone. All of a sudden the body ceases to metabolize alcohol at the old rate. Very disconcerting to those who took pride, however ridiculous, in their tolerance to large amounts.

Blackouts

Excessive alcohol consumption can also lead to 'blackouts', where memory is lost for several hours, sometimes days, even though the subject may appear to behave normally. Why? It's not clear.

One of the most frightening alcohol stories I heard when talking to AA members was of the man who woke up in the cells of a police station, charged with murder. How had he got there? What catastrophe had befallen him and, possibly, someone else? He had not a shred of recollection with which even to begin to patch together the previous 48 hours.

Withdrawal Symptoms

Withdrawal symptoms haunt anyone who has developed tolerance. It cannot be long before you drink again because otherwise you will suffer. And it doesn't have to be the complete absence of alcohol for a period of days that causes withdrawal symptoms. For those with chronically high blood alcohol levels, late in the morning after the night before will be quite uncomfortable enough.

There may be some withdrawal symptoms.

Withdrawal syndrome is the nervous system's reaction to the lack of alcohol. It is believed to represent the overactivity of certain brain regions once they are no longer suppressed by high levels of alcohol in the bloodstream and the brain.

Those who have experienced withdrawal say that there are few things worse. They feel in a panic about the next drink, and pray for some pharmacological palliative. They may well have the shakes and possibly other manifestations, including the particularly unpleasant 'ants crawling under the skin'. Going down the stairs, they tread warily. And the torture isn't just physical: it is the disquieting knowledge that you won't be 'normal' again until you've had a drink – whatever normal is these days.

What has happened to your pleasant social habit; the good times? You know very well what has happened: you got hooked. You are hobbled, imprisoned by booze; at its beck and call. Time to go and see your GP. He can open the door not only to appropriate medication but also to other kinds of help. He may well advise you to check into a private or NHS clinic to be 'dried out'. Drugs used to counter withdrawal are fairly powerful sedatives, including Librium, Heminevrin or Valium used in a reducing dose over a period of five days. Vitamin B is also given. Once the worst physical symptoms are over, it's time to consider things alcoholic and whether or not you should give them up for good.

Medical Conclusion

It seems daft, but alcohol really does have two faces. One with its gaiety, a lubricant for many a congenial, funny evening with friends. The other a mad, sad face pressed up against a hospital window.

The answer is simply to watch it. Too many glasses of wine at too many social evenings could lead to a life-threatening habit. Of course there is a well-worn path from the bar to the hospital bed. Try not to take it. After the initial laughs, it's a dead bore.

And don't think 'drinking a lot' is something crazy like two bottles of vodka a day. A ten-year mortality study from all causes in the USA revealed the following:

- People who had zero to two drinks a day had the lowest mortality rate.
- Non-drinkers and those who had three to five drinks a day had a 50 per cent higher rate than the first group.
- Those who had six or more drinks a day had a 100 per cent higher rate.

♈♈♈♈♈♈♈♈♈♈♈♈♈♈♈♈♈♈♈♈♈♈♈♈♈♈♈♈♈♈♈

This is how I spent the next three years of my life as my world crashed around me. Drinking. Nursing home. Drinking. Nursing home ... I was a helpless alcoholic.

Jimmy Greaves (This One's On Me, Coronet Books).

♈♈♈♈♈♈♈♈♈♈♈♈♈♈♈♈♈♈♈♈♈♈♈♈♈♈♈♈♈♈♈

11. Booze and Relationships

Merry Hearts

Can drink lead to steamy, dreamy sex? Of course it can. Drink and romance and its loving fulfilment go together like a horse and carriage trotting lovers around New York's Central Park. For those with big budgets, there are the first-class restaurants where the champagne or white wine nestles in a silver bucket of ice and the liqueurs are served in cut-glass goldfish bowls. The waiter, ready to pounce on the bottle and refill your glass the minute you have taken a sip, is a little intrusive. But really you are on a bewitching island: inhibitions and uncertainty dissolving in the wine. Mutual attraction magnifies. Soon, mentally, you are eating each other. Can you hold out until the coffee?

On smaller budgets, the effect can, of course, be replicated. The bare wooden table top at the bistro may look a little spartan, but once a big candle has been lit in the middle, making the wine gleam in the glasses, it's perfect. And reasonably priced enough to be able to afford a brandy and Cointreau on the rocks. Miles Davis is on the sound system, another carafe of wine is on its way and, later, will come the lovemaking.

At home you can lay on a veritable feast with the best wine at half the cost of eating out. Candles, background music and excellent food complete the picture. And the bedroom is just upstairs so, with no hovering waiters to worry about, you can always have a break between the main course and dessert.

Then there is the wine bar where hard-pressed male and female executives meet to laugh, flirt, joke and drink their way out of the tensions of the day. The gripes about the boss, the long hours, low pay, lack of recognition. Ouch! Have another? Certainly. Can't go now – just ordered another bottle. Hey, this is starting to be one of those nights to remember. Where will we be at 2 a.m.?

Too Much of a Good Thing

For most people, particularly in romantic situations, drink brings on a glow which lets down barriers, allowing merriment, good-heartedness and sexual attraction to flourish. And that's as true of middle-aged married couples as it is of student lovers. It may be a full-dress dinner, an after-work session in the wine bar, an amble down to the local, or simply putting your feet up and having a drink together at home.

But only so much of what you fancy. Perhaps the man at the expensive restaurant orders another bottle and drinks most of it himself. Having had gins and tonics *en route* should he really finish off with a large brandy? What will happen later? Will it be (excuse the golfing allusion) all swing and swank and no ruddy hit – a non-event? If so, he's going to wake up feeling foolish and angry with himself. And if he's regularly tempted to drown his sorrows, he may soon find himself crossing the line into the bleak category of Problem Drinker.

Perhaps after too many glasses of wine the girl at the bistro becomes giggly and begins to slur her words. Then she starts to apologize profusely, time and time again. In bed? She collapses fully clothed *on* the bed and falls fast asleep.

At home, what starts as a romantic evening is ruined when the wife, after half a bottle of champagne and a full bottle of wine, suddenly starts a character assassination of her husband.

At the pub, we find the middle-aged fellow getting pie-eyed on a strong guest bitter while his neglected wife, nursing a Martini, looks on resignedly. Eventually she goes home alone.

The Hard-drinking Partner

If one partner in a relationship is swimming in booze and the other is on dry land, it can lead to friction – unless the one on dry land is the soul of patience.

And, of course, the roles can switch. One day the man spends an extra hour at the pub. Another day, the woman can spend an extra hour at the wine bar. At home the dishwasher needs emptying. The sitting room is strewn with yesterday's newspapers. The mail has arrived with a clutch of bills, and there isn't much in for dinner, so it's a question of cobbling something together.

Many people believe that drink depresses domestic anxiety, although it has not been the subject of extensive study. At a distance, and after half a bottle or more of wine, you don't care about the state of the sitting room or whether the dishwasher is full or empty. If all there is for dinner is a can of pilchards and a few yellowing pieces of lettuce, who cares? And as for bills …

Well, you don't care until you get home. A woman returning from a few drinks with the girls after work might feel aggrieved to find her partner in a bad mood after doing all the aforementioned jobs and staring rather bleakly at the bills. This contrasts sharply with the jokes and gaiety of the wine bar. Also, there is no wine in the fridge; the magic potion has been withdrawn. And the pilchards are the last straw. The remainder of the evening looms as bleak and lifeless as an Easter Island statue.

Where have the girls gone? Yes, to that new bistro. And that's where she wants to go for more wine, more laughter and a decent dinner. The alcohol is urging her on but she wouldn't admit it.

Where alcohol is, in a sense, unfair, is that it commits people to creating justifications for further imbibing which can be quite hurtful.

Alcohol-fuelled rows can be dangerous, leading to things being said which can't easily be unsaid: performance in the bedroom; the character of each other's parents, brothers and sisters; professional competence; old friends; financial mismanagement.

The 30-day Programme in a 'Drinking' Relationship

You are in a relationship with someone who drinks too much. Do you (a) have a quiet word with them or your doctor or (b) simply turn a blind eye to the stumbles, the loud voice, the glassy eyes?

Going on the wagon yourself for 30 days may prove helpful, but it's not without its hazards. There may be the odd comment from your partner as you pour your evening Coca-Cola: 'I don't know how you can drink that stuff. I'm having a nice gin and tonic, thank you very much.'

There needn't be any confrontation at this stage, but the slight strain between the (temporary) abstainer and the partner is there. And it puts rather a damper on the cocktail hour.

Let's suppose it is the husband who has decided on a month-long break, possibly for health reasons but perhaps he is worried that he has been influencing his wife to drink too much. Encouraging her to match drinks with the boys at the pub is asking for trouble.

His wife knows this is a good part of the reason, but because she is already worried about her own drinking, she finds it an added strain. And it is in the nature of alcohol that although it causes people considerable anxiety, it is also (at first) an effective relaxant. In a mad kind of way, it treats itself: the tension produced by drink is dissolved with more.

The wife who marches up to the fridge for ice and puts together a brimming gin and tonic is saying, 'Let's talk about this tomorrow. Just for now, I'd rather do this,' taking a large gulp.

Making fun of the Coke? Why shouldn't she? She thinks he should mix up a mineral water with ice and lemon which at least resembles a gin and tonic. He could then join in the 'fun' with the illusion of having a 'real' drink.

And more might be expected of 'Mr Temperance'. His wife may exploit his sobriety by having more to drink than usual at the pub or parties, knowing that he'll be safely driving home. She may stay out for drinks after work or go out with the girls and come home slurring her words. Anything to avoid returning home with its daunting new sobriety. But all the time she is working hard at staying out and having a good time, she is avoiding the real question – what to do about her own fondness for drink.

The husband is left feeling out of it and at a loss as to how to tackle the problem. Would things 'normalize' if he started drinking again, perhaps a little less than before? Remember, he's often been the one pouring the gin and making a joke of the large measures he was giving her. Had he often pressed her to have another drink in the hope that she might become more amorous? Yes, he had. And now he is feeling guilty about his wife's drinking. What can he do?

Would 'talking it through' help? Over a drink? Might be worth trying but could lead to a row. The husband is clearly frustrated. One way of dealing with that and getting some useful advice would be to talk discreetly to one or two friends of either sex who might be able to help. But no – not a campaign to try to persuade her to drink less. That could produce real shame and embarrassment.

Sitting down together and talking through the situation seems to be the only solution. To make it work without provoking an argument, the discussion should follow the rules of all good conversation: no taking positions but being fluent, forgiving and understanding. What sort of matters might come up?

- Why has he given up for a month? It was to prove he could do it and possibly provide an example.
- Is there anything wrong with him medically? No, he hasn't even seen the doctor about it.
- Has it been difficult giving up? For the first few days he badly wanted a drink, then the feeling died down rather like a fire going out.

- What did it have to do with her? Quite a bit. She's been drinking too much and it's probably all his fault.

The couple might then go on to discuss how much they normally drink, how often and with whom. They might talk about the drinking habits, including some exploits, of their friends. They may question how much they spend on alcohol and how often they feel under par in the morning. They could discuss what alcohol does to their conversation, their physical contact and lovemaking, all of which have diminished. They laugh quite a lot when they're 'merry' but is it real, relaxed, happy laughter?

A happy ending? Why not? Let's imagine the wife makes a positive decision. No more gin and tonic or straight wine. Instead, white wine spritzers and not too many of those. Or perhaps she decides to try a 30-day programme of her own, with full support from her husband.

Sometimes a fun place, sometimes a testing place, the relationship swimming in too much alcohol can be hell on earth. Apart from anything else, if both partners are constantly out imbibing, they won't spend enough time at home planning and making things happen.

It helps if your partner joins you.

♟♟♟♟♟♟♟♟♟♟♟♟♟♟♟♟♟♟♟♟♟♟♟♟♟♟♟♟♟♟♟♟♟♟♟♟

**If we spent less time drinking and more time think-
ing, we'd be so far ahead we wouldn't believe it.**
Modern Glaswegian saying

♟♟♟♟♟♟♟♟♟♟♟♟♟♟♟♟♟♟♟♟♟♟♟♟♟♟♟♟♟♟♟♟♟♟♟♟

12. Bye-bye Hangover

As a self-inflicted illness, the hangover has no parallel. The name was evidently given to the condition in the 1920s when Dorothy Parker and the epigrammatic topers of New York -'one more drink and I'd have been under the host' – were regularly passing out at the Algonquin Hotel.

Looking forward to a good Saturday night at, say, six in the evening, the drinker recklessly neglects the hard lesson so often taught him by the countless other Saturday nights: that having crossed a sufficiently deep river of booze, in just 15 hours' time he will be wishing he'd spent the night differently. The head will be throbbing, the eyes will be rheumy, the mood depressed.

Among the many murderous hangovers in literature, few are better described than in *Lucky Jim* by Kingsley Amis.

A dull thudding made the scene before him beat like a pulse. His mouth had been used as a latrine by some small creature of the night and then as a mausoleum. During the night, too, he'd somehow been on a cross-country run and then been expertly beaten up by secret police.

A hangover was described by the same author in *Everyday Drinking* as a minor illness which 'deserves respect'. Among Kingsley's recommendations for sufferers was: 'Wash your hair', but does it work?

It is doubtful whether there ever will be a magic cure for a hangover. Indeed, in a characteristically effective demolition job of a new husk-free lager – which its makers claimed 'may result in less of a hangover' – *The Times* wondered whether the extinction of the hangover is really what we want. 'Surely not,' rumbled its leader writer. 'The condition, although painful, is a source of folklore, invention and fear. Scores of aphorisms (about beer and cider, whisky and wine, and their effect when drunk in various permutations) and hangover cures (take a clove of garlic and swallow it with a quart of rum whilst facing west) are rich proof of this. The most central is the lesson a hangover dispenses. Drink too much and you pay a price – again and again and again.'

The Emotional Symptoms

The Times did not mention a specific torment of those who wake up after a night of indulgence: bad temper, inflamed by clumsiness and the crass

stupidity of inanimate objects. Consider these instruments of torture lest we forget the trouble they have caused us:

- The knot in your shoelaces which grows ever tighter as you tear at it with your fingernails.
- The shaving foam which splutters its last when you have only soaped your upper lip; or the can of hairspray which can manage only one squirt.
- The disappointingly cool and shallow bath due to the hot water tap you left running.
- The postman's ring at the doorbell when you are still half naked.

- The heel of your sock which splits as you are tugging it on with too much ferocity; or the ladder you make in your new pair of tights.
- The toaster which incinerates your clumsily cut slice of bread.
- The egg which cracks badly as you lower it into the boiling water.
- And the car. The car is always waiting to go wrong on a hungover morning: out of petrol, battery flat, clutch on its way out – a sort of mechanical mirror of yourself.

All these, and other tortures, wait to scratch further the exposed nerves. They would hardly trouble you on a normal morning, but now they lie in wait like hurdles. The response is a welling-up of resentment, an impotent fury, a feeling of being badly served by the fates, a certainty that you are being singled out for uncalled-for retribution, a dogged feeling of hatred for the world and most of the people in it.

The Physical Symptoms

There is little medical research into hangovers, but the mixture of depression, headache, nausea, fatigue, shakiness and hypersensitivity to noise and light are well worth avoiding.

Headache is the most palpable symptom in the early stages of heavy drinking. This has nothing to

101

do with the brain, however, since the brain has no pain receptors. Any headache pain therefore comes from the nerves of the surrounding lining, skin, vessels or muscles.

It's worth knowing, of course, that some drinks are more heavily loaded with hangover-producing congeners (vegetable, mineral and chemical traces) than others. At one end of the scale, vodka is 'pure' and clear and port is dark and loaded.

Other Aspects of Hangovers

Mixing Drinks

Although many drinkers believe that mixing your drinks is a bad idea, it is not scientifically proven to be a producer of hangovers.

Dehydration

Alcohol does 'dry you out'. Wise drinkers will have one soft drink for every alcoholic one.

Tiredness

Alcohol can send you to sleep, but as it wears off during the night, you can experience restlessness. More importantly, alcohol interferes with REM sleep, the deep sleep of dreams. Robbed of that, you awake still groggy and fatigued.

Hangover 'Cures'

Morning-after cures are legion. Any drink containing caffeine will help constrict the blood vessels in the head enlarged by alcohol, but it won't reduce the level of alcohol in your bloodstream. Eating something helps by restoring depleted blood-sugar levels, the liver having been too busy with booze to metabolize glucose. Exercise can help but not much – and it won't hurry the liver's processing of the booze. A cold shower? A very bracing, punitive shock to the system but it won't actually speed up the exit of alcohol.

Hair of the Dog

Having another drink may seem like the perfect cure if you wish to refill the alcohol receptors, stop the discomfort and postpone sobriety. But this is also a false trail that leads to the dependence everyone wants to avoid.

Delayed Hangover

No morning hangover at all? Don't kid yourself. If you took a bucketful well into the night, this simply means you're still under the influence. You can then, unwisely, 'top up' at lunchtime and put off the hangover till later. But it will come – unless you keep drinking, of course.

All in all, there could not be a better advertisement for turning off the tap for 30 days than the certain avoidance of the hangover. Thirty mornings of reasonably alert – we won't claim joyful – awakenings. No regrets, no thudding between the temples, no dizziness, no depression, no gaping at the money departed from the wallet or purse.

Just morning. And, who knows, a good idea lighting up in the untroubled brain. Almost worth signing up for that alone.

♀♀♀♀♀♀♀♀♀♀♀♀♀♀♀♀♀♀♀♀♀♀♀♀♀♀♀♀♀♀♀♀♀♀♀

Sir, I have no objection to a man's drinking wine, if he can do it in moderation. I found myself apt to go to excess with it ... and thought it best not to return to it. Every man is to judge for himself, according to the effects he experiences ... I now no more think of drinking wine than a horse does.

Dr Johnson

♀♀♀♀♀♀♀♀♀♀♀♀♀♀♀♀♀♀♀♀♀♀♀♀♀♀♀♀♀♀♀♀♀♀♀

13. Why Alcohol Puts on the Flab

Alcohol makes us put on weight like nothing else. It is loaded with calories, which produce energy, but has no other nutritional value. The consequences of this are rather more complicated than is generally realized. It is something that has been studied by the peerless team at King's College (London University) Department of Nutrition and Food Science. And released in this book for the first time.

What happens is this. You have a good, but not over-the-top, dinner of seafood, meat and pasta, bread and butter, salad, ice cream and coffee. And to accompany it, three-quarters of a bottle of wine – red or white. The possibility of you doing anything particularly energetic to 'run off' the meal is remote. You may shuffle round a dance floor, run 25 yards to the nearest junction to hail a cab, then go to sleep and get up in the morning. These energy requirements will be easily met by the alcohol in the wine because this is the source, without exception, that will be called on first.

Alcohol is by far the most active fuel since there is nowhere to store it in the body and it is essentially a toxin which must be oxidized. In terms of energy provision, then, alcohol always comes first, leaving carbohydrate, protein and fat standing – or sitting as the case may be, collecting round the waist. It is, therefore, a major contributor to flab.

'Who's taken my liqueur chocolates?'

Will I Lose Weight in a Month?

Those looking for weight loss can expect some impact from their 30-day programme. Here's a rough calorific guide for booze and for some soft drinks:

Pint of bitter	180
Pint of lager	170
Large gin and tonic	122
Single gin and tonic	72
Pub rosé wine	85
Pub dry white wine	75
Medium sherry	60
Single Scotch and water	50
Standard bottle of Coca-Cola	71
Orange juice	80
Schweppes tonic water	22
Diet drinks (if you can stand the discouraging aftertaste)	0.75–1.8
Mineral water	0

It is tempting to suggest that the greatest contributory factor to flab in Britain is people's inability to resist the ever more abundant and varied supply of food and the temptations of advertising. Not so. National figures show that average energy intake has declined sharply since the 1970s. What's happened is a reduction in daily energy expenditure as large sections of the population have become increasingly inactive – no doubt watching all the hyperactivity on television. But people are still overeating *relative to their low energy requirements.* Consuming alcohol provides nutritionally empty calories which, as we have seen, get burnt up first, leaving the food to be stored as fat.

Giving up for 30 days won't achieve wonders in weight reduction, but you may feel that your waistband is a little slacker. Shall we venture a modest, unprovable, weight loss of, say, five pounds? Ten?

14. Enjoying the Cash Benefits of 30 Days Off

Now this is fun – the positive cash flow caused by negative alcohol. To make yourself aware of the money you're saving, you could simply take less cash out of the bank or put one of your credit cards in a drawer. But it might be more appealing to keep a jar beside the bed and sling in the notes and change that would normally go on daily drinks.

To give yourself added incentive, think of something you would like to treat yourself to with the money you save, and stick a label on the jar, such as:

NEW CD!
NEW NOVEL SIGNED BY AUTHOR!
NEW PAIR OF SHOES!
PAIR OF WEST END TICKETS!
HOLIDAY SPENDING MONEY!
FIRST PAYMENT ON THE NEW CAR!

Use this jar exactly as intended – not just as a repository for small change or foreign coins – and its contents will grow like a chrysanthemum. Even in

30 days, there will be a reasonable pay-back for shunning the booze. Just watch it mount up.

Travel can take your mind off things.

Let's see how much can be saved during a month off. Sally, aged 35, is a recruitment consultant. Her consumption is 'moderate' and she knows when to stop, but she enjoys talking business over a bottle of wine and likes to meet friends and associates in cafés and bars where the chink of glass and the popping of corks beats background music any day.

One day she decides to start a 30-day dry spell. This does not mean, incidentally, that she will shun pubs and bars, and refuse to buy other people drinks. The key difference is that she will not buy bottles of wine for the table and will buy mineral water or Coke if and when it comes to a round.

Let's have a look at some comparisons:

	The 30-day programme	*Not the 30-day programme*
Lunchtime	Two soft drinks £2	Half-bottle Sancerre £4.50
Early evening	Two soft drinks £2	Two gin and tonics £5
Evening meal in	Bottle mineral water £1	A bottle of red £6
Night cap	Drinking chocolate £0.50	Glass of port/ dessert wine £1.50
TOTAL	£5.50	£17.00
SAVINGS		£11.50

Now it won't always work out like that, but people who practise the 30-day non-binge say that a saving of around £10 per day is about right: £300 per month. And you can also chuck in the amount saved on taxis, normally used to avoid drinking and driving.

If your normal consumption is high, you will have certainly saved enough at the end of the month to reach into the money jar and buy something worthwhile: a new outfit, hi-fi, television, a box full

111

'I had no idea he drank so much – we've almost paid off the mortgage.

of new books or CDs, a new watch (if not a Rolex) or a very good long weekend in Paris. Perhaps pay off a few bills. Or, indeed, if you've built up quite a thirst, a case of good wine for later consumption.

15. What to Do with the Time You Save

How much time do you ordinarily spend with a glass in your hand? Half an hour or an hour after work; perhaps a hour later in the evening? And at the weekend, two hours on a Saturday and the same on Sunday – at the pub, wine bar, café, sharing a bottle with friends?

Shall we say two hours daily? That's 14 hours a week – more than a full day out of the seven.

Now the suggestion is not that your 30 days should be spent like a monk in retreat but that you should continue to meet people, substituting soft drinks for hard. Even so, there is room in your 30-day programme for some alternative activities.

Shall we put a figure on it – seven hours a week? That's 28 hours-plus within the 30-day programme to do something different. What to do may be a problem which will be resolved only by drawing up a list. How best to spend this precious gift of extra time which would otherwise be whiled away pleasurably sipping wine and generally having a terrific time?

Resolve immediately to do something that will measurably make a difference. Leave business out of it. Do *not* start a huge report entitled 'How I Would Change This Company If I Were Managing Director'. Start in your own back yard. Here are some suggestions.

Family Life

Spend more time with your partner – an individual, not someone who just happens to be there when you get back from work via the wine bar. What will please him or her? It may be a holiday – a well-planned holiday for once. Or simply a weekend away.

If you have children, be honest – what about treating them less as objects and more as individuals? Instead of running a mile when you see or hear them playing with the computer, picking out chords on the guitar or trying to fly a model plane, join in, show interest. Do you help them with their school work, read to them, sit down and watch a video with them which isn't exactly to your taste? They're your kids; no one else is going to do it for them.

DIY

Okay, scream in derision, but how about hanging a trellis on a bare outside wall? It will repay the effort in the pleasure it gives you, even if fiddle-faddling around with a drill, hammer and masonry nails is not your idea of fun. Think of the unalloyed admiration and envy of your friends; the kudos; the improvement to your property!

Exercise

Admit it – you have often shirked exercise in favour of a visit to the pub or wine bar. Now is the time – now you have the time – to tighten up those slack muscles. Try jogging (if your feet will stand it), cycling (if you have a working bicycle) or swimming if you don't mind getting chlorinated water up your nose. There has been much publicity about exercise releasing the brain's natural tranquillizers, endorphins, but, as with most activities that have a purpose, the main kick is the feeling of accomplishment when the task is finished. That feeling of 'there, I've done it' which you don't get after completing a bottle of Côtes de Beune Villages.

If you are a golfer, decide to do something about your swing. Don't think it will be improved by purchasing a new set of irons, or a new driver. Admit it, you need a lesson from the professional at your club.

Exercise can be a good diversion.

Get Organized

Let's face it – your holiday photographs are in a visual stew. What was that happy group on the beach – you remember the faces but where was the beach? Which year? Here is a job to test the steeliest resolve, requiring half a dozen albums, dozens of labels, the ability to remember whether it was Florida, Antibes, Catalonia or Tighnabruaich, and considerable skills at caption writing. Good for a few quiet evenings at home ... but what satisfaction when the job is done and the years have fallen happily into place!

Car Maintenance

Now the car is getting on a bit, how about giving it a treat and changing the oil? It isn't that difficult. Get some old newspapers, wear your old jeans, buy a few litres of oil, open up the sump, drain off the old stuff and give the old jalopy a new lease of life. Now, doesn't that feel better!

Literature

Read *War and Peace*. Don't let anything put you off – the three names of all the characters, the huge length. Read it as fast as you can. Not to have read *War and Peace* is an insult to literature. When you are in the midst of the Battle of Borodino, you won't be thinking about drink.

'Got anything a bit more substantial?'

Cooking

Take up cooking. Cooking is easy; it just requires concentration and good timing. And the more you concentrate on the food, the less you'll worry about the lack of alcohol. Keith Floyd makes cooking enormous fun, but remember – the accompanying glass of wine is not essential.

Learn a Language

Buy a book, cassette or video and get stuck into French. No, you will never get a job in Paris or Brussels, but it might be helpful next time you have a car breakdown on a lonely road 30 miles from Limoges. How nice, further down the track, to read Maigret in French! It's never too late to start. Astonish the natives; become a true European!

Computing Skills

For years you have been uneasily using a word processor. Perhaps abusing is a better word. Get on top of this deficiency in your education. Find the workbook for your particular machine and get the help of a youngster who can make the thing dance around the room just by snapping his or her fingers. Spend several evenings going through all the basic routines and learning all the shortcuts that have eluded you. At the end of your 'course' you'll have more confidence, having at least partly mastered the technology.

Letter Writing

Write some personal letters (either by hand or on the word processor). The relief at having done this will be enormous. And don't forget to post them.

Learn an Instrument

Choose a musical instrument and take the first steps, assisted by a good teacher if you can.

Are 30 days long enough for any of this? Long enough to make a start!

'I just tell myself, only 10 more days.'

16. Well Done, You Did It!

Well done, indeed! You may immediately feel like cracking open a bottle of champagne, or heading straight out to your local.

But before you do, take stock for a few minutes. Get out a notebook or sit at your computer and jot a few things down. This should be under the heading AS A RESULT OF NOT DRINKING ALCOHOL FOR 30 DAYS, I …

Well, what did you do? You know what you didn't do – and that's spend quite a lot of time drinking. Write down what you feel you've accomplished, and not just bob-a-job things waiting to be done in an idle moment or spasm of impatience. Did you read *The Cherry Orchard*, if not *War and Peace* (next time) or re-read *Pride and Prejudice*?

Did you take a couple of hours to clear out the back cupboard and find, to your delight, some old prints which you thought had been lost in a house move?

Did you write to an old friend in Texas who

replied with some photographs so that now a holiday there really is in the offing?

Did you get a pal over who knows about maintenance and change the oil in the car so that it runs more smoothly – even if only you notice?

Did you spend some of your non-drinking savings on a necessary golf or tennis lesson which has improved your game?

Faced with a particularly daunting work project, did you decide, without grumbling, to haul it home and spend a full Sunday morning on it – with results that dazzled on Monday?

And did the self-improvement extend further than tasks? You should also record your changes in mood during your non-drinking spell. Were you more agreeable? Asked to carry out some simple household task, were you less liable to grumble than usual? Did you instead bounce to your feet and get on with it?

Was your selfishness level way down on the scale to normal? Could this be because you were unconcerned about the next drink, or escaping to the pub?

Admit it – you might have had more time to follow the society you live in. You had more time to read the newspapers, watch the news, tune in to *Newsnight*, get up on a Sunday morning and watch the excellent David Frost. You became more a part of the media swim – though that itself can become an addiction, as you probably know.

So, how does it look? How do you rate yourself? You must, of course, be honest. This may be a programme about taking nothing at all, but it is not without significance. The main thing is that you got through 30 days without a drink. That was the objective. Nothing more or less than that. But there were some side-effects/benefits which you would be a fool not to have noticed. Answer 'yes' or 'no' to the following:

You missed alcohol at first	**Yes/No**
You still missed alcohol in the third week	**Yes/No**
You read a colossal book and enjoyed it	**Yes/No**
You worked hard at improving a game or hobby	**Yes/No**
You got cheesed off with comments about your non-drinking	**Yes/No**
You did some better-than-average work which got noticed	**Yes/No**
You were nicer and more considerate to your partner	**Yes/No**
You lost some weight and feel good about it	**Yes/No**
You saved some money and feel good about it	**Yes/No**
You took some time to write letters and re-kindle friendships	**Yes/No**
You feel good about having carried out the 30-day programme	**Yes/No**

Now see how your answers stack up. There is no winning formula here. But you may feel that, apart from the multifaceted benefit of doing what you set out to do, there have been other advantages which count in your own situation. Only you know them. Only you care.

Calls for a drink, doesn't it? Well, that is entirely up to you.

'His 30 days are up and he's lost the key.'

17. What Happens if You Slip?

This is the shortest chapter in the book. You've slipped. The pint just slid down when you weren't looking, as it were. The glass of wine dribbled past your guard. Well, don't worry too much about it.

You can't, of course, pretend it didn't happen, unless you are one of those people who kid yourself to the point of fatuity.

But don't be too hard on yourself. Spend a few moments going over what went wrong. See if there are any lessons to be learned. Were you pressured in some way? If so, why were your defences so low? What was it that someone said which made you think: 'Hell, just the one; it won't count.'

But it does count, doesn't it? Or is all this just play-acting? Do you abandon other things in life just in the middle because you can't be bothered? No, because you'd let the side down. Isn't it just as bad to let yourself down?

The solution to the slip? Just start the clock again on Day One. And this time, *complete the course!*

Temptation will be all around.

18. What if You Really Can't Do It?

As mentioned in Chapter 1, this is not a book for those who know, or have a fair suspicion, that they have already developed a dependency on drink. But if you can't do the 30-day programme, you had better admit it: you have a problem.

The useful simile of the mountain climber applies. If you know your limitations and take things easy, you will enjoy scaling rock-faces until old age tells you to seek a less daunting hobby.

If, however, you get too ambitious, rush the climb, push your skills beyond the limit, you might have a serious accident that will mean permanently hanging up your climbing boots.

Just so with alcohol. Whether alcoholism is a genetically predisposed illness, allergy or a behavioural phenomenon has been a matter of debate among doctors and psychiatrists for many years. One clear cause, however, is drinking regular amounts of alcohol some way in excess of modest social drinking, plus fairly frequent drunkenness.

Put another way, it seems possible to 'catch' alcoholism and become addicted and hindered by a condition that is progressive – progressively downhill – rather like arthritis.

And, of course, one clear signal that the condition is taking hold is the denial of the individual, to him or herself and to family and friends, that anything untoward is happening. This denial, standing in the way of progress towards a personal solution, is one of the most depressingly inevitable features of alcohol dependency.

Alcohol Dependency Syndrome

In London, Alcohol Concern has an impressive library of international academic papers and publications on the subject. In the International Classification of Diseases, 'alcoholic' has been replaced by the term 'Alcohol Dependency Syndrome', defined as: 'A state, psychic and usually also physical, resulting from taking alcohol, characterised by behavioural and other responses that include compulsion to take alcohol on a continuous or periodic basis in order to experience psychic effects, sometimes to avoid the discomfort of its absence; tolerance may or may not be present.'

The following fairly typical indicator of a drinker's progress to some hard decisions may be useful. It has been compiled with the help of doctors and those who have recovered from alcohol addiction. It is, of course, dangerous if taken literally.

1. As a teenager, you may respond to alcohol differently to your friends. It starts the little people dancing around in the brain.

2. You are more often drunk and *more* drunk than others. The special effect of alcohol is something you embrace; it is like having a special friend. At this stage, it would be difficult for any observer to figure out what are youthful high spirits and what is alcoholic behaviour. You are not sure yourself. No one has told you what to expect and you have avoided health education material on the basis that it doesn't apply to you.

3. You are spending more time than others in wine bars and pubs. Alcohol is invariably present in the system. Lunchtime drinking is topping up. You may be a little disturbed by this but remain true to your 'friend'.

4. You start becoming slow-witted in company – the jokes no longer fly from your lips. You sit with friends grimly trying to remember a funny story but can't quite bring it off. Everyone notices you're below par but no one says anything.

5. You begin to drink alone. You spend evenings drinking a bottle or more of wine gaping at the television and feeling miserable.

6. You contemplate stepping off the kerb and being winged by a bus. A bespoke accident? Anything to break the deadlock. You've got some sleeping pills to help you through the

night. You long for obscurity and small
tasks.

7. You try to give up – and do for a few days –
between binges. When you stop drinking you
start getting worse and worse withdrawal
symptoms. You are sweating profusely. Tremor
is frightening: how can the whole body vibrate
like a tuning fork?

8. About time: you check in to a clinic for drying
out. This combines isolation from ordinary
existence with drugs to help relieve
withdrawal, plus counselling.

9. If you are lucky and determined enough, one
treatment at a clinic is sufficient.

10. Gradually you come back to life, abandoning
your alcoholic 'friend' and, indeed, any flesh
and blood friends whose *raison d'être* is being
in the wine bar. And then you go along to AA
and see if, like millions of others since it was
started in 1935, you can benefit from a contact
and support group *par excellence*.

Getting Counselling

Your own doctor might help as an occasional
counsellor, but he's got breast cancer screening,
arthritic old people, childhood diseases and everything in the medical manual on his plate. Many
find that the only way of keeping up a guard
against a condition which is expensive, injurious to

relationships, tenacious, ultimately life-threatening and unbearably tedious is to go to an AA meeting.

Alcoholics Anonymous

There are 3,000 meetings of Alcoholics Anonymous attended by about 50,000 people in the UK every week. Sufferers need only pick up the phone and find out the nearest meeting to them – often held, for economy, in school or church halls.

Are they anonymous? Yes, they are. You don't have to give your name or sign anything.

Do they cost anything? There's no fee, just a voluntary collection towards tea or coffee and the hire of the hall.

Do you have to chant, or pledge anything? Decidedly not. The 12 Steps of the AA Recovery Programme are suggested, not foisted on you.

How do you qualify? You simply have to want to stop drinking.

What happens? The huge success of the AA programme is the formula of a short address by a member who has been dry for at least two years, followed by a sharing session where difficulties are ventilated. The key is that those who have made progress encourage those who are in the early stages. The core belief of the programme? That normal life can be restored, and enhanced, by abstinence from alcohol. In other words, once you've fallen badly off the cliff face, best not to go up again – find something else to do.

As the AA handbook rather eloquently says:

For most normal folks, drinking means conviviality, companionship and colourful imagination. It means release from care, boredom and worry. It is joyous intimacy with friends and a feeling that life is good. But not so with us in those last days of heavy drinking. The old pleasures were gone. They were but memories. Never could we recapture the great moments of the past. There was an insistent yearning to enjoy life as we once did and a heartbreaking obsession that some new miracle of control would enable us to do it. There was always one more attempt – and one more failure.
The less people tolerated us, the more we withdrew from society, from life itself. As we became subjects of King Alcohol, shivering denizens of his mad realm, the chilling vapour that is loneliness settled down. It thickened, ever becoming blacker. Some of us sought out sordid places, hoping to find understanding, companionship and approval. Momentarily we did – then would come oblivion and the awful awakening to face the hideous Four Horsemen – Terror, Bewilderment, Frustration, Despair …

AA can and does guide people back to peace and fulfilment, but no one pretends it's an easy road. All of which is a very good reason for taking it easy – keeping your drinking within safe limits and practising the 30-day programme once a year. Or more often if you feel like it.

It's your liver; it's your equanimity; it's your life.

♀♀♀♀♀♀♀♀♀♀♀♀♀♀♀♀♀♀♀♀♀♀♀♀♀♀♀♀♀♀♀♀♀

People who are the type of alcoholic I am, whatever that is, are afraid of a boring life. 'I guess now it's all downhill.' Well, it isn't. You find that you are perfectly capable of having a great time – and you can get so much more done.

Grace Slick

♀♀♀♀♀♀♀♀♀♀♀♀♀♀♀♀♀♀♀♀♀♀♀♀♀♀♀♀♀♀♀♀♀

Your 30-day Calender

Number of days	Tick for no alcohol
1	
2	
3	
4	
5	
6	
7	
8	
9	
10	
11	
12	
13	
14	
15	
16	
17	
18	
19	
20	

Number of days	Tick for no alcohol
21	
22	
23	
24	
25	
26	
27	
28	
29	
30	